Zen

and the

Art of Negotiation

Zen
and the
Art of Negotiation

**Successful Negotiation for People
Who *Hate* to Negotiate**

Philip L. Marcus

The Silloway Press

Columbia, MD

Zen and the Art of Negotiation:
Successful Negotiation for People
Who *Hate* to Negotiate
Copyright 2010 Philip L. Marcus
All rights reserved.

Printed in the United States of America.
ISBN-13: 978-0-9802057-1-8
ISBN-10: 0-9802057-1-9

Library of Congress Control Number
2009941932

For Peg, my constant companion and cheerleader, without whom it would never have started, and once started would never have been finished.

Acknowledgments

No one writes a book all on their own, least of all your humble (really!) and obedient servant. At the very least, there is the legion of authors of books one has read and people one has known and debated with and learned from. But they are a multitude. So I will only try to list all those who participated directly.

I begin with my son, Dr. Gary Marcus, a professor of cognitive science at NYU. First, he wrote a book, in fact several of them, demonstrating in a close-at-hand way that it was possible to do this (notwithstanding the millions of books written before). Second, and more important, he wrote *Kluge: The Haphazard Construction of the Human Mind* a couple years ago. One of the points made in *Kluge* is that the seemingly unitary business of decision-making in people is no such thing, but actually done by two parts of the brain and in very different ways. That is a key foundation of this book. I am deeply indebted to Gary for this and many other ideas in *Kluge* that underlie especially chapter one here.

My daughter Julie Marsden is a young adult, some 46 years younger than I, well embedded in the "Millennial" generation. Frequently, the differences in language and culture between us become apparent. (How can she possibly be texting while carrying on a conversation with me?) She was the inspiration to start thinking about what happens when crossed generations try to work out deals, as she and I often must. I thank her for connecting me with the differences while trying patiently to deal with her hopelessly out-of-date dad.

Kluge came out at a time when I was thinking about how people make deals, both in formal business situations and less formally in boards and legislatures. About the same time, I read an article in *Negotiation Journal* called "A Logic for the Magic of Mindful Negotiation" by Darshan Brach, Esq. So things converged. I am also indebted to Ms. Brach for bringing them together.

There are two primary pairs of authors whose books have influenced my thinking about negotiating deals. Roger Fisher and William L. Ury introduced the idea of non-adversarial negotiation in the 1981 bestseller *Getting to YES*. Ronald Shapiro, Esq., and Mark Jankowski have written several books, of which the most important to me was *The Power of Nice*.

Once I began writing I desperately needed feedback, not so much about style and grammar—that would come—but about whether what I was writing made sense and was useful and well organized for the reader. Often it was not, and that valuable feedback was provided by a friend named Angie Boyter. Her advice was invaluable in making the structure of the book.

Stories pin down the ideas of a non-fiction work. I reached out through a service called "Help a reporter," http://helpareporter.com, for people with negotiation stories illustrating my points. Many people responded, but I must acknowledge those who had the most crystalline stories and whose I therefore used: Lynn Jordan, Steve Krefman, Esq.,

Marlene Waldock, Catalan Olteanu, Eric Stamos, Debbi Mack, Esq., and Andrew Cagnetta.

Even those who think they can write need an editor. I think I can, but I owe much to Kathleen Silloway, a skilled editor whose eagle eyes prevented me from publishing many incomprehensible sentences that made perfect sense to me, as well as grammatical errors that would have sent me back to third grade. Thank you, Kathleen.

Finally, if Peg and I were not married and she were not a publisher I doubt I would have undertaken writing a book. It would have loomed too large. But her patient explanation of what happens, and what happens next, and next after that encouraged me to keep on clickin'.

Contents

Introduction

Do you hate to negotiate? Maybe you have a good reason. But this book can help you.

Those who negotiate regularly—like lawyers, sales people, high-level managers, diplomats, and politicians—have developed tricks, skills, and techniques, and a comfort zone where they feel less stress than other people when negotiating. Having been through it so often and maybe having taken courses, they are prepared emotionally. Would you be as ready to hit major league pitching as a major league batter is? Or would you see a 100 mph fastball coming and just bail out of the batter's box? You probably don't have the training or experience to handle that pitch.

Actually many people who think they rarely negotiate do so every day. What? Sure. You negotiate little things, like who at home will take out the trash, walk the dog, etc., often in exchange for other tasks. The same is true in the office or shop.

Or maybe you are on a committee or the at a school, a faith organization, or a charity. You often negotiate with other members about what actions should be taken and (too often) about those little procedural requirements people abuse to get their way on policy. You horse trade with other members or let one hand wash the other. This is all negotiating; it's just in a little bit different environment than some think of.

But because these occasions are so casual, unless you pay attention you may not learn any negotiation technique. Those who consciously negotiate often have the advantage, because they are always thinking about the process of negotiation.

I wrote this book because I know there are plenty of negotiators who badly need help, either because they don't often negotiate, or they think they aren't and don't focus on learning how to negotiate. They need the help just **to balance the experience and skill often found on the other side.** I remember when I was starting as a trial lawyer, and had little idea what to do to settle a case for my client without accidentally selling them down the river. I didn't know the art. It was many years ago, and there was no one systematically studying negotiation from different aspects. There were no books I could turn to.[1]

Over the past 25 years, however, there has been systematic multi-professional study and there now are plenty of books on how to negotiate. I have read many of them. While I walk here on the shoulders of giants like Bill Ury and Ron Shapiro, their books are mostly for a person entering one of the careers

---

[1] For subjects not covered in law school, I did read Francis Wellman on *The Art of Cross Examination* and books on accounting for lawyers, etc. But it was another decade or more before really useful books on negotiation technique began to appear.

that require frequent negotiation, or for someone reviewing or enhancing existing skills. They are not aimed at the occasional negotiator.

This book takes some of the academic knowledge of the past 25 years plus some new ideas of my own and breaks it all down so you can use it. It is not a treatise. You will not find a lot of footnotes, although there are a few, and is not full of examples and proofs, although there are some good war stories. The style I hope is light and easy to absorb (or use as a refresher). The chapters are mostly short and always to the point. I want it to be just plain usable.

A personal experience finally stimulated me to write the book. A friend was beginning to negotiate a separation from her husband. (No, she is not my wife.) Although represented by an attorney, she was still in a sea of anxiety, facing a husband who had learned to manipulate by growing up with a dominating mother and surviving. My friend is a professional, but negotiation is not consciously a big part of her work life. I was able to give her a guide through the storm by teaching Zen mindfulness and by helping her put some things in perspective.

What came through was that the most reasonable person, when confronted by an emotional situation such as a negotiation with large consequences, has their reasoning overthrown by those emotions. They get to their "Impulse Place." They often know it and then they hate it, but don't know how to get out. This book is here to help you learn to control your emotions in a negotiation and to rationally weigh costs and benefits. It is also to teach you to have a plan for negotiating to a deal you can live with—so you will no longer hate negotiating.

Let's get started.

one

How Your Zen Space Can Help You Negotiate

It's very hard to get your heart and head together in life. In my case, they're not even friendly. —Woody Allen

Fear, impatience, and other emotions make people hate to negotiate, and make them do a poor job of it.

Controlling emotions is part of my overall method or philosophy of negotiation. And it is the core part. I am not going to just tell you to "snap out of it" (what a useless piece of advice). This book will show you how to both control your emotions—your Impulse Place[1]— by entering what I call your Zen Space[2], and then how to plan and carry out the steps that will lead to a sustainable deal that is at least close to your goal.

Imagine many people's worst nightmare, going to a new car store to buy a car. Wow, you are

---

[1] Impulse Place is the cross street at the end of Lonely Street, where Heartbreak Hotel is located. Sorry, Elvis.

[2] The first recognition I know of Zen mindfulness as improving negotiation is in an article in the *Negotiation Journal*, vol. 24, no. 1 (1/2008) by Attorney Darshan Brach called "A Logic for the Magic of Mindful Negotiation."

going to be pounced on by a hungry salesman or saleswoman ravenous for a sale. They have been trained with all the tricks to get you to buy what's on the lot—preferably the car that has been baking for six months with no nibbles. He or she is going to get you to pay too much and to feel honored they were even willing to sell you a car. And once that part is done, you are going to visit...the finance person. Once done there, you will be so confused with arcane terms and weird numbers that you will pay anything to get out of there. And anything is exactly what you will pay.

Do you feel that churning in your stomach? It's your lunch, yearning to be free. But you can't let it go. You need to look cool, no sweat, tightly controlled although you are as tight as an overstretched drumhead, ready to rip. But still not as tight as the muscles in the back of your head, giving you the worst ache you ever had. Boy, are you ever ready to bargain with a professional and get the best of him. Ready to ... bow down to the god of cars and sacrifice your next paycheck and the one after that...and....

Sorry, but I had to do that, to get you into your Impulse Place^{SM}, where reasoning takes flight and emotions rule. OK, take a deep breath, because this book is about relief.

Being in an emotional state causes people to make mistakes of reasoning, and causes them to be impatient for a resolution so the emotional pain will goes away, often at a time when patience is exactly what will bring about a desirable outcome.

Being in control of your emotions allows you to handle things I will tell you about in this book that you need to do. They include listening to your worst enemy with an open mind, listening to your counterpart berate your skills and berate what you propose to sell or your offer to buy. I will teach you to resist stating a "negotiation position" (an offer). They will include keeping your cool while sometimes your counterpart espouses values you hate. How do you do all this? I will teach you how, by leading you to your Zen Space^{SM}. That is where, without chill pills, you can keep your cool.

There is something besides just keeping your cool. The Zen meditation technique allows a person to find truth. Not just big truths like, "What is the purpose of life?" but ones a little smaller, like "Why do those whack jobs on the other side of this political argument have such nutso ideas?" In other words, the technique helps you open your mind, or become "mindful."

Of course, I would not put these expectations and demands on you without teaching you how to handle them. In all cases, you will do that by entering your Zen Space[3], which you will learn about in the next chapter. And I will ask you to practice a great deal so that this all becomes second nature. Negotiation, like all skills, gets better with practice. As you read this book, and re-read parts that need re-reading, you will do well to *practice* the Zen techniques. You will know you have arrived when you go to a movie in a theater not to watch the movie but to watch you watching the movie. This may not make sense now, but it will by the end of the next chapter.

---

[3] What everyone else calls "mindfulness" I call your Zen Space, just to put a brand on it.

§

I do not believe that using tricks or ploys gets you to a sustainable deal. Tricking or coercing someone starts you on the route to a deal that breaks down and may even end up in court, as one side or both accuses the other and refuses to perform. Still, refusing to depend on tricks and ploys is a forward-looking view that not everyone shares. So many negotiators do employ tricks to frighten or anger you that you need to be able to parry those emotional threats.

And since I recognize that you may face them, I will arm you to deal specifically with tricks and tactics. That armor also requires you to get in your Zen Space. So what is it, why do you need to get there?

Today, science can demonstrate that there are not one but two parts of the brain that deal with analysis and decision-making—one automatic and fast and crude, and the other slow and methodical. The first—which some people call "reflexive" because it is like a reflex—is influenced greatly by one's emotional state. There is a second or "reflective" part of the brain that is calculating, methodical, slow, nuanced, and little influenced in its outcomes by your emotional state. Shortly, I will present some of the scientific evidence for two brains, as well as a brief history of meditating to reduce stress and do better decision-making by putting the reflexive brain in charge. But wise people have always known this intuitively.

I have put more detailed information on this into Appendix A, for those who want the scientific details.

It's about the history of Zen and how people, including scientists and others, think it works. It describes the history, early and more recent science developments (including neuro-anatomy) that bear on the benefits of a Zen or meditative approach.

Of course, you can use the information in the rest of the book without knowing the science that makes it work. If you can work hard at the techniques without the underlying science then it will be fine.

Negotiation, like all skills, gets better with practice. As you read this book, and re-read parts that need re-reading, please *practice* the Zen techniques until they are fully a part of you.

Let me make this clear: I believe in negotiating while being in a careful, reasoning mental state, and I believe in the help Zen provides in getting to that state. Still, I do not believe that it is desirable to be constantly in the super-rational state that makes negotiation effective—not reacting to fears, desires, anxieties and other emotions that overwhelm. By no means.

One must be aware of one's feelings to be in touch with one's humanity. That was the point often made by Mr. Data in *Star Trek: The Next Generation*. No great art—visual, musical, or any other form—and no great love would be possible without feelings and emotions. They are a key part of life. Understanding how out-of-control emotions may be influencing people you are negotiating with can be very useful. Still, being under their influence is not useful to *effective negotiating*.

A suggestion: As you work your way through this book, compare what you would do in negotiating situations with what other people do—in what you observe in your life and your friends', on TV shows and in movies[4], and in negotiations that play out on the news. Try to understand what people did, why they did what they did, what they might have done better, and what mistakes they avoided or fell into.

§

Finally, negotiation is, although with real consequences, also a game. It has an aesthetic like baseball, basketball, chess, etc.—worth watching on its own terms. Speaking of games, let's take a look at a non-negotiation game. I use it here to illustrate how irrational human thinking tends to be—and as an incentive to you to become more rational by investing time and effort in the coming chapters.

So let's play the "Ultimatum Game." The referee has ten dollars to divide. He is going to give you some of that money. The game will be over, and the ref will give us each what I propose, but only if you accept what I suggest. If you reject my proposal then the game is also over, but neither of us gets anything. Simple game, right? Ready to play?

I will give you two bucks out of ten, take it or leave it. I get eight and you get two. OK?

Psychologists and other scientists have run this game 100s of times, and the two-dollar offer is often rejected. How can we explain this? After all, it may not be a 50/50 split, but you would get two bucks instead of nothing. This rejection is not exactly rational, but it actually happens about half the time. What's up?

---

[4] They are lousy models, but why are they lousy models?

The UG is one of many games and decision situations studied over the past couple of centuries, initially by economists. They are very interested in making models or simplified representations from which they can predict human behavior in making decisions with money outcomes. These models are word and number descriptions of human behavior in large groups. Games, the economists think, can help them reduce decision-making to elemental ideas they can use to make their models.

The models generally assume that people make decisions between alternative courses of action based on a *rational* evaluation of their consequences. The standard models include the "expected utility model" for decisions with uncertainty or risk, and the "discounted utility model" for decisions with consequences spread over time. (It is called "discounted" referring to the "discounted" value in money *today* of a promise to pay X dollars say *a year in the future*—discounted because you lose the chance to put the money in the bank during that year and earn interest.)

These models have the advantages of being explicit in form and workable for analysis. They are mathematical. You can use them to make predictions in precise number form about decision-making in a wide variety of circumstances. And you can use a computer to help calculate the results with various inputs. So the models have provided a strong and attractive foundation for economists to develop theories about decision-making, while assuming that decisions reflect the operation of a single all-purpose information processor, like what a computer might do making decisions.

To economists' chagrin, the models often fail. Human decision-making just does not follow these rational models. You think otherwise? How well did you do with the two-dollar offer in the Ultimatum Game?

Let's play another game. I will give you either fifty bucks in hand or a coin-flip chance on 110 bucks. (Note: This is a mind game. Please do not send me an email asking for your money.) Which do you want? Most people take the $50 in hand, but it's a bad choice.

Any expert in probability and statistics would point out that if you do this more than a handful of times, you can expect on average, with multiple tries, to get 55 bucks if you always go for the coin flip. (They call $55 the "*expectation*.") But people shy away from the uncertainty, a phenomenon called "*loss aversion.*"[5] The behavior violates the economists' discounted utility model. So much for pure economic models.

What's going on? I talk about anatomy, neurology and the like in Appendix A, all of which support this. For now, though, let me discuss why this irrationality matters when you negotiate, and what some Buddhists and their followers know and do about it.

First, in negotiating with someone, you are trying to make a deal or bargain with him or her. Ordinarily

---

[5] Someone I discussed this 50/55 game with said, "The 'Irrational' decisions may BE the most rational—it would be very rational for me to choose $50 certain over $55 maybe if I am flat broke and hungry." I replied that it was very clever but was an addition to the circumstances of the game, and that the bereft state, not the hunger, made the sure $50 a more rational choice then. What do you think?

they will make proposals, you will make proposals, and perhaps some combination will be acceptable to both. Of course, there are many factors that go to whether a bargain is struck and, if so, how long it takes. These factors also affect what happens afterward, and there often is an afterward—a time during which each side has to deliver some money or goods or services to the other. But each side must analyze both its own and the other side's proposals and ideas.

So, what can *interfere* with a computer-like exchange of proposals, analysis of proposals versus needs, making counter-proposals, and so forth? First, one side may be so distrusting they don't even want to meet with the other. There may be a rational basis of distrust, such as prior betrayal of trust or breach of promises. But often the distrust is at least partly irrational. It can be based on the innumerable reasons people do not trust each other, such as race, religion, appearance, accent, where they are from, their age, and so on.

Second, we are also influenced by prior experiences, often not really connected to the current bargaining. "That guy looks like so and so, my enemy in grade school; I cannot trust him." "That woman looks like my best friend in college and so I should believe exactly what she says." How about, "Last time I was in a room painted that shade of green I embarrassed myself, so I had best be on my guard."

Third, we know from the "50 or 55 game" above that fear of uncertainty has a very large effect on decision-making.

Fourth, we often unconsciously account for the expression on the other person's face, trading in skepticism for the approbation of a smiling face. (If you want to sell something, smile at the prospective buyer.) What else accounts for some of the successes of politicians who have no business making policy for the rest of us?

Fifth, when we are trying to make a deal and uncertain about what will come of the bargaining, we get anxious—impatient to get to the end. That very impatience can cause us to accept a bad deal just to get it over with. Professionals know how long it may take, are OK with waiting, and will take advantage of the amateur they sense is impatient.

I am going to stop counting problems now, because any positive or negative prior experience with a person, a place, a thing, a scent, a sound, or any other sensation can bring to mind more irrational reasons to be influenced in decision-making. This is not a new revelation. Humans are not good (rational) decision-makers, although they can be fast. As I said earlier, there is detailed material on the scientific basis for this in Appendix A. For the moment, let me outline just a little history of the meditative approach to finding truth and reason.

§

Beginning probably in the fifth century, a few people in China began to meditate as a way to knowledge, influenced by various branches of Buddhism. In fact, the word Zen is Japanese for this form of meditation, called in Chinese *chán*—

with similar words in Korean, Vietnamese, and other Asian languages.

Although the origins are shrouded in the uncertainties of unwritten history, it is clear that Zen Buddhism differs from other branches of Buddhism in that it turns its back on religious texts and verbal discourse as paths to truth. Zen focuses instead on the idea that truth is found inside oneself, by isolating oneself from the outside. Thus, maybe paradoxically, one finds knowledge about the here and now by cutting off thoughts about past and future, and about what might be and might have been. In English, this state is often called *mindfulness*. So, one meditates in the hope of finding truth through mindfulness—what I call entering your Zen Space.

The Zen Buddhists were by no means the first to practice this meditative state. There are references to Hindu meditation in writings going back more than 2,500 years. The Old Testament—associated with Hebrews or Jews—refers to meditation, and monastic Christians have practiced this since the beginning of that religion. Meditation is also an essential feature of the practice of the Religious Society of Friends, or Quakers. Islam, going back some 1,300 years, makes meditation a central part of its five-times-a-day prayers.

More recently, for almost 100 years, physicians and others have recommended secular meditation for reducing stress, pain and other symptoms.

A related state to meditation, called *hypnagogia*, describes that state entered between wakefulness and sleep. As early as Aristotle, people have written about this state, as did Edgar Allen Poe much later. Everyone who has thought about it knows this state, but there was no scientific study until the early 19th century.

The hypnagogic state often features fantasy images or geometrics and auditory sensations ranging from ear ringing to imagined snatches of speech. When the state is entered in the presence of another, such as a therapist, many people experience increased suggestibility similar to outright hypnotism. That is, someone can be induced into a hypnagogic state, with restful sounds and images, and then "walked through" examinations of their feelings and reactions, etc., under direction, as a means to more effective talk therapy.

Whatever may be the similarities and differences between meditation and hypnagogia, it is clear that mental states between wakefulness and sleep offer opportunities to explore and experience what wakefulness usually blocks. And paradoxically, wakefulness seems to allow a pre-rational or reflexive part of our brains to take over if we are stressed, preventing rational analysis of risk and reward, pressing us to act primarily on feelings—and to act impatiently. This is good when a lion or mugger is running toward you, but not so good in a negotiation. A state "below" wakefulness can help the more rational, analytical, slower part of the brain to take over.

OK, this is not scientific proof. But isn't it enough to make it worthwhile that you go on to chapter two to read about a mindfulness technique—to engage the slower, analytical "reflective" system while doing negotiations that may have a large impact on your life?

As one final incentive, let me tell a fairy tale. We all know the story of the Three Little Pigs. The first pig built a straw house; the wolf came and blew it down, and so in a panic the first pig ran to the second pig's house. It was made of sticks, the wolf blew it down, and both panicked even more and ran to the third pig's house. It was well planned and well built,[6] designed while the third pig was in a rational state, and the wolf failed to blow it down. He eventually fell in a cauldron of boiling water and became lunch instead of eating it.

This somewhat gruesome tale reminds us of the benefit of careful planning and of not panicking. Panic—the Impulse Place—is a negative feature of the primitive or *reflexive* brain. Careful planning by your *reflective* brain is aided by getting in your Zen Space so you can out-think tricksters and bad guys.

In chapter three and the following chapters, I will talk about how to negotiate once you are in a mindful state or Zen Space. You will need this Zen Space to do what you will learn in these chapters. Without it, you will panic or become impatient or otherwise screw up. Are you ready to learn how to get there? Let's go!

---

[6] It probably followed modern building and zoning codes, and neighborhood covenants.

two

Making Zense of it All[1]—
Getting to Zen Space

It's [the Web] a great medium for trivia and hobbies, but not the place for reasoned, reflective judgment. Suprisingly often, discussions degenerate into acrimony, insults and flames.
—Clifford Stoll, Silicon Snake Oil, 1995

As important as this chapter is, you will find it rather short. Sometimes big ideas do not need a great deal of expression to state them effectively. Einstein used a brief expression to show that energy and mass (substance) could be converted back and forth, one to another—an idea startling for its time. Still, one can easily do the relevant computation using third grade math. The idea was simple. Of course, the implications are enormous, both in science and in international relations.

The implications of being able to bring your mind and body into a state in which your reflective mind dominates over your reflexive are also pretty big, as we will see.

---

[1] The author is fully responsible for this chapter title, which was used despite the good advice of the editor and the publisher.

The basic thought in this book is that many people come to negotiations in a state of anxiety, worrying about what the outcome may be, and often believing their negotiating partner[2] is an ogre or devil. They may have other anxieties as well, such as a fear that they will leave money on the table and disappoint the folks whose interests they represent. They are in their Impulse Place.

Impulse Place is my term for the state in which one is prepared to deal with an emergency, the example often given being a sabertooth tiger suddenly seen not far off in the forest. Epinephrine (adrenaline) pumps, and you get ready to fight the beast or run from it—fight or flight.

Actually, there is a third option, when fighting is futile and flight is likely to fail. That is hiding.

Find a big tree and get behind it, hoping the tiger has a cold and will not smell lunch, i.e., you. Often in life, the hiding option is the one people select, saying nothing and letting the beast lumber past. It may be combined with other tactics such as throwing out a decoy piece of meat, which is also known as *appeasement.*

In the very short run, these three options—fight, flight, or hiding—are useful, but simply selecting from the three does not make for a good long-term strategy, one that balances the benefits of foraging in the forest with the possibility of encountering a predator.

---

[2] In this book I use the term "negotiating partner" for the other side of the negotiation. Whether that means the entity on the other side or their representative(s) will be clear from the context, but usually it means the entity.

How do we get into a mental "space" that will counteract these negative and panic-laden feelings, make us feel happier with negotiating, and promote rational discussion across the table?

You would do best to start when you do not need to get there, just as the time to learn to run shouldn't be when your building is on fire. You can best come to this technique when there is nothing anxiety-producing going on, no reason that will keep you from being able to get comfortable physically, away from distractions, in a room by yourself, telling your roommate or partner you will be taking a nap.

Go ahead, close the door to a room where you are by yourself, put on some quiet music—something that will fade into the background but help you ignore room sounds, noise from outside, and so forth. Sit in a chair that can recline or at least allow you to recline.[3] Dim the lights a bit, because visual images can also be distracting. If you have some mild pleasant incense, you can burn it and make your olfactory sense comfortable. Please close your eyes for the moment.

OK, squirm a little. You first position is never exactly right, is it? Take a few really deep breaths. It's amazing, isn't it, how rarely we just think about breathing deeply. We don't usually have the time. So take the time now. Take deep breaths that you think about rather than just letting your brain do them automatically. Doesn't that feel good? Death

---

[3] I do not recommend lying down on a bed. You don't get to your Zen Space by sleeping, and if you are healthy, you are somewhat conditioned that lying down is associated with sleep.

is about not getting enough oxygen to your organs,[4] and it is worthwhile to think more about breathing deeply than we usually do.

Think about how many of us are always alert to making money—opportunities, to-do lists, threats to our happiness and security, enemies. Isn't that all nonsense in the long run? For the time being, throw it all out of your mind.

Instead, imagine in your mind's eye a scene you make up that includes no one you know, nothing frightening or even all that interesting. I like being on a boat gently floating down a river, with a soft spring breeze, the smell of flowers but no strong scents. But you can imagine anything you would like. Try different scenes until you feel relaxed—not a care in the world.

Pay attention, again, to your breathing. That's it; in...out...in...out...breathing gently but fully. What are you thinking about? You don't have to figure anything out. Just recall your relaxing scene and how nice it feels to breathe gently and fully.

Be careful, however, to remain awake. If you feel you are going to sleep, just open your eyes or move a bit. Your Zen Space is between full wakefulness and sleep, closer to wakefulness. You are aware of the outside world, but not focused on it, nor concerned with or anxious about it.

Some practitioners recommend using progressive muscle relaxation.[5] Here is how. (If you have

---

[4] Really. See *How We Die* by Sherwin Nuland, M.D., in which he explains this.

[5] This is a method developed by Dr. Edmund Jacobson in the 1920s. Some nice videos on the web take you through the procedure as a supplement to what is here. Google "progressive muscle relaxation."

movement restrictions, modify the following, and do not do anything you find painful.) Use the same comfortable room as I have just described, but start by tensing your feet so they cannot move. Now let them go, so your feet begin to float. Go through this alternation a couple times, leaving your feet relaxed. OK, now alternately tense and relax your legs, leaving them relaxed or "floating." Tense your stomach muscles, and then let them go and repeat this, leaving them relaxed. Do the same with your arms, lifting them to tense them and then gently letting them gently down. Alternate a few times and leave your arms relaxed and floating.

Good. Next, tense your shoulders, and then let them relax. Do this for a few alternations, ending with your shoulders relaxed. Now lift your head a moment, hold it, and then let it down gently. Twist it gently from side to side. Repeat a few times, and end with your neck relaxed. Ah, doesn't that feel good? Isn't it good to feel good?[6]

By a combination of breath concentration and progressive muscle relaxation (and no mind-altering substances), you will be able to get to a relaxed state in which you are not asleep but not your usual nervous, anxious self. It may take a little practice, but it is the rare person who just cannot get there. So keep practicing. And don't worry if it takes a few tries.

---

[6] Some restaurants play music with "driving rhythms" which encourage—not a relaxed state—a tense state that invokes reflexive thinking. I suppose their idea is that fast music will get you to eat fast and finish your meal, so new customers can occupy your table. Don't they realize they may be causing you to have indigestion, which will not bring you back to them, or even to pick a fight with your server?

Pretty soon you will be ready for the next step.

§

Just lie there now, taking it all in, how you feel, what things sound like, your breathing. Now go ahead and think about some problem you have been having with someone, or once had. (The first time I did this, I "conversed" with my father, who at that time was half a dozen years beyond actually being able to converse with anyone.) Imagine that person, call them X, but realize they aren't really with you. So you can say anything you want.

What would you like to say to X? What do you imagine X saying? And your response? Are you feeling tense a little? Take a few deep breaths and focus on them again. Say (in your mind's ear) what you would really like to say to X. Don't be nasty, but don't hold back. Feel yourself taking charge. Doesn't that feel good? Tell X everything you think about your relationship and its history. If they interrupt, tell them you aren't finished. What do you think such a conversation would be like in real life? Would you be able to be as in charge? What do you think would really happen? What is the worst that could happen? How would that feel to you?

Try "talking" with X again and say what you want but imagine X doesn't say the nasty, manipulative thing you expect. How is that possible? Oh, because you are controlling the conversation! Maybe you can do that in real life. Now, once again, think about your breathing, in and out, in and out. Listen to the music and notice how good you feel. Now begin to come slowly out of this trance-like state. When you are awake, think about what it was like.

§

That was a good first experience. What should you do now? Don't stop. This is very much like riding a bicycle. The first time was a bit difficult, but it will get easier and eventually you will be able to do it without thinking about it.

Your next session probably should not be the same day as the first, but soon. Again, prepare the space for sound, light, and possibly scent, and arrange not to be interrupted. Again, breathe slowly in and out three or four times, paying attention to the flow of air and the time it takes. If it helps you, do a progressive muscle relaxation.

Again, after you have settled in, have an imaginary conversation or negotiation with someone with whom that has been difficult. This time, try to have a longer conversation, and imagine how X will respond to what you say. Don't reject what X says out of hand. Respond, but try to figure out why what X is truly saying. Does it have mostly to do with what X says is in his or her personal interest? Does X necessarily try to over-reach or harm you?

It's not only about you, is it? Can you understand that better in this relaxed state? You see, when you are not focused on detecting and dealing with dangerous animals and people, you can think much more clearly. That is what we call being in your Zen Space.

Please repeat this several more times, allowing each experience to occur more closely together. Each session should take about ten or twenty minutes.

§

Let's see now whether you can get to your Zen Space without having a special environment of quiet and subdued light. Try just closing your eyes and thinking about your three breaths in and out. Do some progressive muscle relaxation. If you have practiced, then you will probably be able to get there in your own home. Eventually, you be able to get there in reasonable public places. ("Reasonable" does not include being in the audience of a rock concert.☺) The key is to practice, even when you can arrive in your Zen Space reliably. This way, if you need it, you have it.

three

The Sustainable Deal

Magnificent promises are always to be sus-
pected. —Theodore Parker

Everyone knows that the way you get a good deal is
to lie, cheat, threaten, and/or intimidate, right?

Obviously, there are people who use exactly these
techniques to get what they want. I would be lying
if I said otherwise. I claim, however, that these are
not good long-term strategies, and in a moment I am
going to show you the evidence. First, though, I need
to define a few words, mostly to exclude a few things
from being "deals."

Hundreds of years ago, when you bought a piece
of land (with or without any structures, which were
considered to have minimal value anyway), the seller
would go out on the land with you and scoop out a
clod of earth from the land and hand it to you, the
buyer. He would do this after you had paid him the
money you had earlier promised to pay. This charm-
ing ceremony was called *[de]livery of seizin*, and is
reflected today in the passing of keys to the buyer of
a house or car.

I bring up these deliveries only to kick them out of the way. These final acts are what lawyers call conveyances, handing ownership from seller to buyer. In land transactions today these conveyances are done by *passing papers, closing, settlement, closing escrow*, and other regional names, that preserve a little local color in America (until Starbucks or McDonald's starts conducting settlements). My point—and yes, I have a point—is that **none of these is a bargain, deal, agreement, treaty, or contract**. They are *deliveries*, often of piles of papers, even in the simplest automobile transaction. The *deal* to buy the car was done earlier, in that magical miasma facilitated by new car smell and impenetrable finance terms.

A contract (or deal, bargain, agreement, or treaty) is always an *exchange of promises*. "I promise that two days from today I will come back and give you thousands of dollars and one of my kids, and you promise you will deliver to me a brand new PowerMobile."

Most contracts, especially commercial contracts, call for repeated deliveries, often of various goods in exchange for deliveries of checks in the mail. Most contracts are exchanges of promises to deliver something, such as goods or money. What do you think happens if one side of a contract bullies, lies, cheats, or threatens to get the other to sign a contract? The victim will screw around with delivering whatever it has promised to deliver. That is true even if all the victim needs is to obtain financing and then come to settlement. You would be surprised how hard it is sometimes to apply for financing...when you think you got screwed in coming to the contract in the first place.

Even if the deal is with a criminal organization that promises protection in exchange for weekly payments, the shopkeeper who "promised" to pay them may well happen not to have the money, or otherwise do a lousy job of fulfilling their bargain. Or they might call the police to be waiting next payoff day. A contract to pay "protection" is not very **sustainable**. Neither is any deal where one side feels it was tricked or bullied into agreeing. Nor is a deal in which one side feels it has been forced somehow to compromise ethical or similar principles.[1] On the other hand, a deal where both sides believe the other acted in good faith, although maybe not giving in on every issue, is likely to be carried out pretty much as written. It will be sustained.

When one side makes threats or uses good cop/ bad cop or other tricks, the other side probably will find ways to screw around. Psychologists call it "passive aggressive" behavior. I call it an "unsustainable" deal. It is not the kind of deal that leads to predictable results for the people who made it, and predictable results are the only kind that are good for business.[2]

---

[1] Medical personnel of certain faiths, for example, feel strongly that certain medical procedures or drugs are contrary to their religious principles. There is an entire literature on this subject, including a chapter in *Compromise and Integrity in Ethics and Politics: Splitting the Difference*, by Martin Benjamin. Congress and state legislatures have also stepped into the controversy, with legislation either enforcing or disabling these views when balanced against the needs of patients.

[2] Racing and the stock market depend on the uncertainty of outcome, except they do depend on racing tickets being paid off for winners and shares being delivered by buyers to sellers, and eventually returning to value if they crash.

Zen and the Art of Negotiation

This short chapter is to set a scene. Next chapter I will go into strategies for making deals, and I will always have in mind **sustainable deals**. Unsustainable deals brought about by lies, cheating, bullying, etc., are not worth the effort to make them. I am not going to write about how to make an unsustainable deal. It will only end up with both sides teed off and maybe lobbying or suing.

four

There's No Negotiation Like Strategic Negotiation

Strategy is buying a bottle of fine wine when you take a lady out for dinner. Tactics is getting her to drink it. —Frank Muir

Any well-thought-out plan for business, a military campaign, or even the purchase of a new TV, will include a strategy. In fact, it will have:

A goal that leads to ➤
  A strategy that is implemented by ➤
    Appropriate tactics.

Your goal could be to sell your farm called Whiteacre for at least $10 million for straight cash at settlement. Or to drive from D.C. (near where I live) to Portland, OR (where I am thinking of moving). Or your goal may be to get a particular model of plasma TV.

Your strategy is the general roadmap to your goal. Here is an example. In driving Washington, D.C., to Portland, OR, I might decide to drive generally westward, using interstates where they are available, or else other four-lane highways, and using two-lane highways only if nothing else is available. The **strategy serves the goal**, never the other way.

As for tactics, staying with the example,[1] I might start on I-270 from the D.C. Beltway (I-495), then get on I-70 at Frederick, MD, and stay on I-70 until I hit Western Pennsylvania. Then switch to I-76 East of Pittsburgh, then onto I-80 near Youngstown, OH, and stay on I-80 all across the Midwest to near Ogden, UT. Then get on I-84 through Idaho and on through Oregon to Portland. Each choice of route is a **tactic, and chosen to serve the strategy** in the previous paragraph. Of course, I might run into local weather conditions, needs to stop for sleep, food, pit stops, etc., that might take me temporarily on lesser highways.

Tactics are flexible actions, again chosen **each to carry out a strategy**. Strategies are carefully chosen and then not altered without good reason. Tactics change with conditions. Strategies generally do not, unless you find your strategy is massively in error and is going to have you end in L.A. instead of Portland. Strategy should always implement the goal. Don't create or modify one without this in mind. Certainly do not modify the strategy to justify doing tactics that happen to come to hand.

Why such rigidity? It isn't rigidity, it's discipline and focus. It keeps you on track to implement the goal and not waste resources on a seductive tactic just because it is cheap or easy to do. This discipline applies to conducting a negotiation for yourself or your constituency.

---

[1] You may want to Google "Maryland map" to track my tactics.

Someone I know suggested the end step in going from goal to strategy to tactics should be: "Does it feel right?" I think an appeal like this to intuition is quite correct when there is enough experience to support valuable intuition, but not in your first negotiation. Beethoven and Bach learned the rules of music composition before they started experimenting with what just sounded right. You will do best if you are disciplined the first few times out, then go on to test against intuition—but never leaving out the planning stage.

§

Why am I going on about all this goals, strategies, and tactics stuff? Because my experience is that, in any effort to deal with other people who have other ideas (even if they are on the same "side" as you), if you have not thought all this through, the result will be either failure or chaos.

Without a definite goal and a strategy to achieve it at hand, what do you do when you sit down at the bargaining table after shaking hands? What do you say? What is going to happen? The frequent bargainer you are up against has a goal, a strategy, and probably a few opening tactics, all in hand. If you do not have a goal, they are going to take charge and for sure will get the best of the bargain.

A goal? You mean like "Get the best possible deal I can," or that famous boxer's vow not to pay a lot for his new muffler? No, that is like a bag of marshmallows.

I mean something definite—for example, a sale price, terms of payment, and time line for payments and delivery. Experienced negotiators know enough to think this through and debate it with advisors and lawyers before bargaining day, and then write it down. But then the other side might see it. Good. So they know what you want. They are about to tell you what they want anyway.

Then you have to make a strategy to get that goal. What might the strategy be? At the least, regardless of the goal, it will be to:

- Gain as much information as you can about the negotiating partner.
- Exchange visions for a good result with your counterparts. Announce no "position."
- Agree to work for fairness in the result.
- Avoid the two monsters you will soon learn about in this chapter.
- Remain aware of the WHO—What Happens Otherwise (also discussed later in this chapter).
- Avoid demonizing each other and maintain civility.
- Work together to form an agreement that as much as possible includes the points of both visions.

In the rest of this and the remaining chapters I will talk about each of these parts of a good negotiation strategy.

§

I am going to use a term and its abbreviation very often from now until the end of the book, so let me introduce it right now. It is *negotiating partner*, or *NP*. By negotiating partner, I mean the other side of the negotiation, the other side of the table.[2] I do not mean the people you are working with on your side. (If you are an agent or representative, the side you work for constitutes your *constituents*.) And usually I mean the individual or organization on the other side, not its representatives, agents, lawyers, or other spokespersons. (Sometimes the context will make clear I include the representatives.)

§

They say knowledge is power, and I agree. So take the time and effort to **prepare for your negotiation**. (This does not mean calisthenics, although I would recommend always being well rested and properly nourished.) No, I mean that, after defining your goal, find out as much as you can about both your NP and whatever representatives have been employed or engaged by the NP. What you know about a person's or organization's history and current situation could well prove valuable

---

[2] Some may object that a "partner" is always someone on your side, while the other side is an enemy or someone to be distrusted or tricked or intimidated. It should be clear by this point in the book that my experience and that of those who have studied this discipline scientifically shows that this type of demonization is counterproductive. What succeeds is partnership in finding solutions to differences.

in making proposals, or in deciding whether they represent the best your NP can do.

Learn about their styles. Are they fair? Bombastic and intimidating? Supercilious or oily? Paired as good and bad cops? Often playing some other game? Rational or irrational?[3] Check Google for stories about them and, if the deal is important enough, pay for additional information. Also, ask your friends and people in your business.

Find out about the company you are dealing with—what are its current situations on cash and inventory? Read the business section of your local paper or of a national paper such as the *Wall St. Journal*, *New York Times*, or *Washington Post* or their websites. Each of these can help you understand where your NP is strong or weak. Not enough cash or too much inventory is information you can use to your benefit.

You can never have too much information. The only question is how much it will cost in time and money to acquire it and analyze it. We will talk soon about how to use the information. But first, let me digress a moment to pass on a story about the importance of information, from Lynn Jordan of Los Angeles.[4]

The short of it is she went to a hospital E.R. on her doctor's advice to get an I.V. antibiotic. Despite a "Cadillac" insurance plan, the hospital and E.R. docs billed her after insurance some $7,000. It took

---

[3] Many authors about negotiation treat it as a game played by rational players, but this assumption about rationality may be a bad assumption, depending on who your NP is.

[4] She tells it in video at
http://www.youtube.com/watch?v=wRsBFACxbB4.

her a couple of years to get that amount down to about $600. The journey was all about finding out her rights as a patient (under the HIPAA law) to an accounting statement of what Medicare would have paid, called a "UB-04," which is a good measure of the fair value. She also got an independent "patient advocate" to translate the hospital's odd billing codes into standard ones, which revealed double billing and vast overcharging. The bottom line—and I have found this in my own practice—is that often looking in to the details of a claim for money will reveal many errors, oddly usually to the claimant's benefit. It may save you hundreds or thousands, and patience and attention to detail are your allies.

§

How do you exchange visions?

At the beginning of this chapter, I spoke of a goal of selling Whiteacre for $10 million cash at settlement. Would I say this directly to our NP—the folks across the bargaining table? Probably not, at least not in detail at the very beginning. They might well take that as an **opening position** that is subject to negotiation. It is not. It is the limit my side has set beforehand as the point at which it will walk away. That is very different.

I do **not** recommend stating a position as such at all, because doing that invites an auction.[5] You

---

[5] What I call an auction some academics call "bargaining," where only a price is to be decided, nothing else. They distinguish bargaining from negotiating, where several variables are to be decided. Whatever.

know: going back and forth, each side degrading the other and hoping to get the other to yield. An auction is mostly a test of will power and intimidation. You know that from the last time you bought a car.

At this point, I would like to remind you of the title of this book, *Zen and the Art of Negotiation*. You are in a real or imaginary negotiation. Doing that requires you to function with your rational risk/reward part of your brain. It is not a trance, but a mental state of calm and rationality. So I recommend taking a few moments to get in your Zen Space. Then I will talk about what to do to negotiate once you are there.

Even if your NP requests or demands your "position," you demur.

"It is too early in our discussions and likely to be misinterpreted. I believe in communication that is as open as possible. I believe in ending with a deal as objectively fair to both sides as possible. I hope you share these beliefs. If not, this negotiation will take a long time."

Why open "communication," and about what? It should be about what terms matter to you and asking for a similar disclosure from them. "We are somewhat flexible about the selling price, high sevens to low eights, but are in no position to extend credit on our part. What terms are important to you?"

"Ah," you say. "Now they will know you need cash and will dangle cash but far too little." They may, but you have two answers.

"Well, we appreciate your willingness to get your own financing, but the offer of $2 million is not going to lead to a deal. We have investigated pricing on comparable buildings the past year or so. Perhaps we should engage a professional appraiser to put a fair market price on the building."

"I hope our not being able to offer seller financing did not mislead you. We are not in a position where we need immediate cash. Rather, we are unwilling to extend financing that might stretch the deal to 10, 20, or even 30 years."

Candidly, many negotiating partners may bridle at this unaccustomed approach, believing an auction is the only way to go, the only way they have ever gone.

"Yes, an auction is often how it is done. Where it ends depends very much on things outside the realm of fairness (like who can intimidate or flim-flam the other), and also too often focuses on price. It risks not giving enough focus to terms of payment and delivery, warranties, and other important features of a transaction like this. Would you please share your general vision of what this deal might look like when done?"

I would summarize this portion of a typical effective negotiating strategy as **describing** somewhat piecemeal **the vision of your goal for the deal and leading the NP to describe theirs.**[6]

What good does that do? An important part of negotiating is making proposals to the other side. How can you make a useful proposal without taking in account both your side's goals and theirs? If you keep proposing only what you need, then you will probably never make a deal and will have wasted everyone's time, effort, and money.

So, it is perfectly proper to tell the NP something like "I need to have some idea of your vision of a good deal so I can make appropriate proposals—I don't read minds any more than you do."

Sometimes it takes quite a bit of effort for one side to accept that its NP has a very different vision. This story comes from Detroit patent attorney Steve Krefman:

> I was involved in an exclusive license nego-tiation 10 years back where my team were frustrated with the fact that we wanted a license into our current field of use only, but the technology owner wanted us to take a broader license and commit to commercial-izing the technology in another field that was clearly out of our core competence. We had repeatedly told them that we had no intention of entering that other field, that they were welcome to license others to do that, and that

---

[6] When I say the *vision* of a goal, I mean a mental picture of it, but I am not making some tricky distinction between your goal and your vision or picture of it. You may treat them as the same for practical purposes.

we would not commit to entering that field. On the plane out to visit them for the third time, we decided that we would politely stop all negotiations if they raised that issue again. They did. We did.

Though we hadn't planned our specific behavior, it turned out to be a classic. We were seated at a long conference table, with our team members on one side and their team members on the other. All of us had our Franklin Planners open and we were all taking notes. One hour into the negotiations, their team leader made a comment about the pricing we had discussed being workable but only if it were part of comprehensive deal that included our commitment to manufacture products in the new field of use.

Our lead negotiator put down his pen and interlaced his fingers and, in sequence, the rest of our team laid down our pens. I could see a stunned look on the faces of the opposing team, but their leader kept going, extolling the supposed benefits to us of changing our business plan. Our leader sighed and closed his Franklin Planner, and, like a wave moving through a stadium, we each sequentially closed our planners. This time, their leader noticed. His eyes and the eyes of his team followed the wave like a synchronized dance team.

After a few moments of silence, our leader invited them to an early lunch and limited the subject to friendly small talk. Whenever they tried to talk substance, we discussed weather, travel plans, their products, and the stock market—anything but the deal. After lunch, they asked for a short private meeting. When they returned, the negotiations resumed without them ever raising the deal breaker issue again. Their prior lead negotiator took a back seat in the remainder of the discussions.

The take-home lesson: It is pointless to repeatedly make proposals that are completely at odds with the NP's vision.

Or is it? When there is such a large difference, one side is going to have to yield if they want a deal.

George Mitchell, former Vermont Senator and now recognized international mediator, brokered a deal between the Protestant and Catholic sides in Northern Ireland. The Protestant vision was consistently a disarmed Irish Republican [Catholic] Army. The Catholic side insisted that would never happen, much because they viewed the U.K., which controlled the territory, as leaning Protestant while claiming neutrality. The Protestants of course said no deal was possible with an armed opposition in existence. The impasse dragged on for years, as did the violence.

Mitchell believed no deal could be had until a formula could be devised for eventual disarmament of both combatant forces. He kept asking the IRA political wing if it would agree to disarmament, and the answer for years was "no." Finally the continuing violence, involving combatants, police, and non-combatants, induced two women—one on each side but working together—to demand a deal. A formula was found for gradual disarmament in exchange for gradual increase in local political power, shared by both religious factions. The peace has held, a sustained deal.

Sometimes asking for your vision in the face of repeated "nos" pans out—if you have the patience and the reason to keep bargaining, or little reason not to. In the Northern Ireland case, of course, people—outsiders—came up with a vision that included not only a snapshot of a disarmed IRA but also a kind of movie of the steps that ended up there.

As a picture has multiple features, a negotiation goal has many features. Some are more important than others are. Some are even *sine qua non*—without which, no deal. Do you tell your NP? After all, if something is your deal breaker, why would they not just say no to it or demand a high price?

Why not, indeed? Because they want a deal, and saying no prevents a deal. If they want no deal, you are bargaining with the wrong folks. Move on. If they hold your deal breaker hostage, then figure out theirs and hold it hostage. Soon enough both sides will decide to behave more like adults. Or...the other side may propose something that they can live with, something you didn't think of, that gives you a close equivalent of your *sine qua non*, and thus makes a deal possible.

Should you present a vision of your needs that seems unattainable or absurd? So long as it is not illegal, why not? Give the other side a chance to say "No," or make a counterproposal, or even say, "Yes, provided...." Here is a set of examples, provided by Marlene Waldock of BecauseWeAreWomen.com.

> Ms. Waldock was putting together a women's empowerment symposium, and asked a catering company for free lunch for almost 200; a printer for 150 copies of a 35-page workbook; and an actor famous for her TV role in a 1960s/'70s "police procedural" to speak gratis. The caterer did free lunch in exchange for an introduction and mention on the seminar website and in the workbook, and for the exposure. The printer agreed, in exchange for 10 free tickets (marked as $99 each), an intro, and a logo on the website. The actor, who had asked for $5,000, agreed to appear gratis in exchange for exposure and the chance to pitch her then new book.

> Who woulda thought?

§

After the idea of exchanging visions of a deal, maybe even before that, the next point I would ask your NP to agree on is fairness—the idea that **the final deal should be as fair as possible to both sides**. "Can we agree that one of our objectives in this negotiation will be to make the final deal as fair as possible to both sides?"

Almost everyone thinks they are fair-minded, even criminals and despots, although others may not agree they are—and they may not agree others are. If this goal of fairness is agreed to up front, and it almost certainly can be, it becomes a touchstone for the process, and an important one.

For example, one may then suggest that values of properties be based on objective outside databases and appraisers, or on other established or generally accepted methodologies. This saves a good deal of wasteful haggling. The Web has made available, often at low cost or free, a wealth of information on not only items like comparable properties, salaries, etc., but also accepted techniques for evaluating things like going businesses.[7]

Someone asked me what to do when you have very little leverage. Let's say you are dealing with "Whack-a-Mole-Mart," a giant consumer retailer whose business model is to press their suppliers unendingly for lower prices in return for the suppliers getting their goods into its stores. I think there are two answers. The first is to analyze carefully whether you will be making a profit if you give them the price they demand. If not, thank them for their time and start pitching to Arrow, a chain that caters to customers interested in some service along with reasonable prices.

If there will be profit, then remind Whack-a-Mole-Mart that they have already agreed that fairness is important, that this is one of the Midwest values prevalent in their headquarters, town, and

---

[7] That is, neither a business starting up or one near to liquidation.

state. You share that value, and want a fair price so you can be fair to your workers, and also be honest when you promise to always timely deliver their orders to their distribution centers. I would not hint at these ideas, but be polite and forthright in expressing them.

§

In an earlier chapter I mentioned the importance of patience. Some regular negotiators refer to the "dance of the buyer and seller." The idea is that a deal is not going to be struck right away, even if it is just a matter of agreeing to a price that has been recommended by a neutral appraiser. Almost certainly, that price is above what the buyer expected to pay or at least wanted to pay, and less than the seller wanted to get. Each needs psychologically to prepare for the unwanted and yet wanted inevitable result. It is unwanted because the price is wrong for each, but wanted because it ends things—with a deal.

This story was told me by Catalin Olteanu, manager of a logistics company in Timisoara, Romania:[8]

I'd been once in China, trying to buy a fake Rolex. A friend of mine, with some more experience in dealing with the locals, offer to help me. So we went to the shop, and met the lady who was usually selling such things. As we were in a hurry, my friend told the lady to

---

[8] With apologies for the English of a Romanian in part conveying a Chinese person speaking broken English.

speed up and give us the normal price, as we do not have the time to play all the roles...

"Hey, please go fast forward"

"What u mean? Ha?"

"Look, I ask you to decrease the price, you say no way, I pretend I am leaving, you act like coming to bring me back into discussion, I ask for another price, you give me a better price, I am telling you to struggle more, you tell me about your family, economy, bla bla, I tell you about mopai (police), etc...Finally you give me 38 0rmb which is reasonable, I buy and go."

"What this meeean? Cannot do thaaaat."

"Why, is something we do every time, I only need it faster this time."

"OK, only this time, but next time we back to normal, okeeeey?

The dance of buyer and seller was explicitly recognized by both, across cultures. They put it aside because someone had to catch a plane.

§

Still, some NPs or their representatives are just not going to play nice together. Some are about "I can win only if you lose." I am picturing not only an overbearing male but also a female who intends to beat you by being wily. They are only two of the character types you might meet.

Either way, there are two likely outcomes if you think this is going on. One is that you will keep on warily truckin' and eventually make a deal that is reasonably fair—or you will walk away disgruntled.

If you stick with it, then the trouble may only be beginning. In the previous chapter, I spoke about the **sustainable** deal, and this is one that might not be. "I can win only if you lose" might be the road to dispute or even litigation. So you, your boss, or your constituency need to figure out how important the deal is to you. Is it worth the future hassle? Or is it so important you have no choice but to make a deal? Think this through carefully and act accordingly.

§

The concepts of avoiding hostility and working together toward a solution are so important they get their own later chapters. Bullies, Tricksters, and Nut Cases get a chapter of their own by name. But avoiding two lurking sibling monsters is both important and concise enough to mention now:

Beware of these two monsters:

- "If I ask for too much, you won't like me and you will walk away from dealing, and my boss/spouse/constituency will hate me."
- "If I don't insist on enough, I will leave

money on the table, and my boss/spouse/ constituency will hate me. "

Keep in mind that negotiation is **not** about your NP liking you,[9] or about avoiding hate or pain from your boss, your spouse, or the people you represent. If you negotiate to have the NP like you, then you will be simply doing their bidding. It is called being a "sycophant."[10] If you feel yourself in the clutches of this monster, it is time to find your Zen Space and think about the effect of working to have the NP like you. I am not saying, by the way, to take steps so they will not like you. Just do not make concessions for that end. Instead, make concessions that get you concessions from the NP.

§

There is another point about strategy concise enough and important enough to discuss in this chapter. It is to be aware of the WHO; I am referring to the What Happens Otherwise.[11] What happens if you cannot make a deal? It is important to consider this seriously **before** your first meeting with your NP, as part

---

[9] Unless you run roughshod over your NP—and they are not likely to put up with this—your side may well feel you did a bad job. They may be so unfamiliar with the process of successful negotiation that they think you are there to beat up the NP. Dealing with your own side is so important and often so difficult that I have devoted a whole chapter to it, chapter 8.

[10] My editor wouldn't let me call it "kiss-ass."

[11] The professional literature, as well as lay books, call this the BATNA or Best Alternative to No Agreement. I happen not to like the *sound* of BATNA, and think it is hard to recall what it stands for, so I replaced it, just like that.

of preparing strategy. *Can you buy what you want from someone else or sell it to someone else?*

If there is no deal in your business or personal dispute (e.g., divorce), there may next be a court case. What do you expect the court case to look like? Do you understand that the judge or jury may not see things as you do? It may be hard to believe, but experienced lawyers will always tell you that they have unexpectedly lost cases that were extremely strong and won some that were equally weak. So expect the unexpected. Every general or admiral will tell you the same thing about war. *Can you handle the results, both mentally and financially, if you lose a court fight?* Can you afford the direct expense and the indirect expense of your time and that of your associates in preparing and testifying? A court case that you lose may be your WHO. Are you ready for this, or should you keep on negotiating?

Without a doubt, your primitive, speedy, but irrational reflexive brain—once it makes up its "mind"—will insist that if it is to be war you cannot lose. This means you need to figure out what the WHO is while you are under minimum stress. In turn, you must do this long before you get to the bargaining table. The same is true if you are negotiating a business opportunity, such as with a vendor or customer. What Happens Otherwise, if you do not make a deal? What are the consequences? Decide and reckon this in a quiet moment in your Zen Space, before you start negotiating.

In fact, either way, get into your Zen Space, talk with your advisors and consultants, and make sure you fully understand the down side. Evaluate it realistically, not too harshly or too lightly. Write it down so you can read it later and be reminded. Carry this WHO in your briefcase as you sit down with the other side.

The other side also has a WHO, so you should try to figure it out. There is information you cannot know about them, but you can figure out what other vendors they might use if you are trying to sell them something, or how scarce potential customers are if you are buying. Make sure they are aware of their own WHO and that you have analyzed it, but don't press so hard they become defensive.

§

It's time to summarize what we know so far about negotiation strategy.

Strategy serves a goal, the goal you set up at the very beginning. It is a brushstroke plan to get to the goal. This strategy or route to your goal should include organizing an exchange of visions of a good deal and an agreement to aim for a fair deal, understanding the WHO for each side, and some things I have saved for later chapters. (Beside these, they include demonization, and working for a sustainable deal and a workable common ground.) And your strategy includes remaining in or returning as often as needed to your Zen Space so you are always working with your rational brain.

Your tactics should always support your strategy, no matter what seeming shortcuts or other seductive "off-road" tactics might occur to you. In other words, don't take the two-lane road that looks much shorter on the map, unless you like risking a broken axle 100 miles from the nearest cell phone tower.

five

Getting Along is Everything

Civility costs nothing and buys everything
—Lady Mary Wortley Montagu (1689 - 1762)

Negotiations often happen between people and groups hostile to one another but who are forced to deal because of circumstances. They may have very different political ideas, or they may be religious groups with very different ideas and possibly long histories of warfare. Commonly, it is a husband and wife who once loved each other dearly. These are situations where one might not expect negotiation to work, yet it can.

What these situations have in common is difference based on strongly held values. Also, usually each party sees the other side as the devil. They address each other as demons, at least outside the negotiation room, and sometimes inside, too. There are no magic pills to take to cure this hostility, other than the "tincture of time." But there are helpful ideas for at least coming to a deal with each other.

The first is to **begin acting civilly**. That means no unkind words, even while you feel very unkind. It does not mean to actually love your enemy—that is a trick of mind that is probably super-human. But you need to bite your tongue when it feels like it would be OK to call the NP a son of a bitch.[1]

I don't say this is easy. Humans—and I include myself—seem to become suspicious of or hostile to people who so much as part their hair differently, let alone have different ideas. And when they really have acted in the past with enmity and violence... well, let's just say that I know how you feel.

Still, it is not hypocrisy if you can achieve civility. You are not saying to this enemy that you like them, only that you will refrain from throwing knives for the time being. But even that is asking a great deal. How can you achieve it?

I wrote this book in part because confronting actual enemies, and people with different interests or views, automatically invokes the reflexive part of your brain, your Impulse Place. Again, that is the part built to deal with enemies and threats. It does that rapidly but crudely—mostly by choosing fight or flight or hide. It does not do well with solving problems or dealing with people by reasoning.

Therefore, it would be good when you enter a room with your "enemies," or NPs you have not met before, to spend a moment getting in your Zen Space. If you have practiced a good deal, you can get there just by taking a few deep breaths after sitting down at the

---

[1] This is a reminder: your negotiating partner or NP is the **other side**, not the people on your side that share a vision and strategy.

table. This is a big reason I advocate practice—lots of practice—at getting in your Zen Space.

So, what do you do if you cannot get in your Zen Space, for example, because of something the NP or a representative said? You need to find neutral territory and promptly.

[You] "Pardon me; I need to attend to something personal."

[NP, worst case] "What? We are in the middle of this discussion."

[You] "Nevertheless, I need to attend to something personal." [Standing up]

[NP] "What could be so important you need to interrupt us?"

[You] "As I said, it is personal." [Walking toward the door]

At this point, either your colleagues will pick up the discussion or, if you are negotiating by yourself, things will stop. It takes two sides to bargain. Now, find someplace neutral, like a bathroom, sit down, and breathe deeply several times. The hyperventilation will calm you down, and if you have practiced and are focusing on the breathing, you will get in your Zen Space. Mindfully, you will realize that the NP has been baiting you to try to make you lose your cool. It is just a trick, and you do not need to take the bait. You are OK. You are in control. Now you can return to the conference room and resume, of course thanking everyone for their indulgence.

§

Sometimes your grievances against your enemy are warranted, but not always. You will recall that in the last chapter we talked about doing research about your NP. This can now come in handy. As you know, things are not always exactly as they seem. Please stay in your Zen Space for this example:

As of this writing, North Korea—the DPRK— and most "western" nations are at odds over DPRK tests of nuclear and other missiles. At least that is the western view. The history of Korea suggests from their point of view they are justified in what they are doing.

A little research easily shows that Mongolia controlled Korea during most of the 13th century and part of the 14th. It was not pleasant for Korea. There were 200 years of peace before 1850, as Korea successfully isolated itself from all outside influences. Then western powers tried to force Korea open to trading, using "gunboat diplomacy," which is a true oxymoron. Of course, that trading was mostly to benefit the West.

Japan had invaded twice in the 1590s and then thoroughly conquered Korea in 1910 and kept it until 1945, the end of World War II. Then there was war between northern- and southern-based Koreans in the late 1940s, with the South backed by the UN and United States, and the North backed by their Chinese neighbors and the Soviet Union. There was a truce in 1951, but no peace treaty has been made.

With all that violence it might not be so surprising that North Korea is paranoid about more invasion, and has built a large army and nuclear weapons.

My point is not for you, the reader, to become a great friend of the North Koreans. They are adults, and are responsible for their actions and their often bellicose threats. Still, it is useful when dealing with this mentality to bring to the bargaining table an understanding of their history—why they act so wild and woolly.

That standard, of expecting adult behavior from both sides while understanding the other side, is often useful in more mundane bargaining. And it helps in getting the gist of some new research on values-based disputes—where the two sides differ on core values.

A recent study[2] tells us something interesting about values-based disputes such as the current one between the DPRK and other nations. Proposals based essentially on buying off core

---

[2] Reported in *Negotiation Journal* as "Reframing Sacred Values," Volume 24, Issue 3, pages 221-246 (July 2008), published for the Harvard Project on Negotiation by Wiley.

values with economic benefits do not work. An example of "buying off" is that a country might offer North Korea free or cheap grain for stopping nuclear development. This has been tried, but they often take the grain and soon go on developing. They continue to nurse their need for strong self-protection while accepting tons of grain as their due—as a reparation. They seem not to have accepted the sincerity of the various nations' food and humanitarian aid. That may be because those nations' media publish repeated sneering stories about North Korea's self-indulgent head of state and their tragic economic condition.

Proposals based on apparently sincere efforts to assist the other side in solving a problem may work, as may sincere apologies for past transgressions. Renunciation of past misstatements of fact is often helpful. Phony apologies, however, make things worse. (The complete result of this study is beyond the scope of this book. But imagine what you would want from someone who had trampled the core values of your town, company, religion, or other group.)

Imagine someone offering you money to betray your mother or father. When you refuse, they offer you more money. You protest that you love your parent and that love and protection of parents is a fundamental value to you, taught from childhood. They display no interest in this value but offer still more money, mixing their offers with veiled or open threats. How far do you think this "negotiation" might get? (How far has the United States gotten by repeatedly increasing the price on the head of Usama bin Laden?)

Imagine instead someone taking a different approach. They might start by acknowledging your love or at least respect for your parent. They then state they have similar, albeit not identical, values. They say that unfortunately and without your knowledge your parent has done a bad thing, one that your basic values would agree is bad. And they need your help to undo the bad thing or punish your parent. There is no mention of bribes or threats.

In fact, the bigger the economic offer, the more likely it will insult the one getting the offer. This is one conclusion from the recent sociological data, reported in the footnoted journal article. What can work, with time, is being willing to listen respectfully to the values of the other side and the consequences as seen by that side. One can listen without agreeing.

Let me repeat that. Just because you listen to someone, and even understand what they are saying and why they say it, does not mean you agree with them. The more comfortable you are in your own skin, the more comfortable you will be looking at the other person's skin, warts and all. You can do this from your Zen Space, where you are comfortable with looking intensely at the other side's views. If you can do it without antagonism and acknowledge what they believe, then you have taken an important step toward a successful negotiation. There is no loss of face or strength in saying, "While I do not completely agree, I do understand what you are saying."

On the other hand, some people are very hard-headed about not understanding what you say, not wanting even to hear it, or putting it down. You may have some people on your side of the table that refuse to understand or even listen to the other side. Often that is because they are very uncomfortable about themselves. They are what psychologists and similar professionals call "defensive." They are defending themselves against ideas scary to them by constructing barriers out of words. Defensive people have a hard time building trust with NPs and coming to successful, sustainable agreements. Offer to buy them a copy of this book if they will read it.

You will feel more comfortable about yourself and less defensive if you are in your Zen Space. You can get to it by doing the exercises in chapter two. That is why you will be better off if you practice often, so you can get there quickly and reliably. In your Zen Space, you can grasp this:

> "You are strong. You were able to get safely through the vulnerable time when you were a small child. You learned that you are separate from other people and have the right to have different needs and to have different ideas about how to live. Just because you understand their needs does not mean you give up yours. You learned all this in your first three or four years, and it is still true today. You need not defend yourself. You are doing nothing wrong."

Some points reveal themselves here. First: No matter what, do not express hostility at the bargaining table. It cannot possibly help. You do not need to like someone to work together, either to solve a problem or resolve a dispute. You need to be civil and listen to them even when you totally disagree. Listening never implies agreement. If you are too pissed off to talk civilly, and this can happen to anyone, excuse yourself from the table.

Second: If you feel good enough about yourself, and even if you are not prepared ever to accept their values, ask your NP nonetheless to fully express their values, including the ones that involve fearing, hating you, or even accusing you. You can learn a lot and maybe better understand what they need and seek and why.

A third point, far hazier—maybe not even sharp enough to be a point—is the idea that the overwhelming majority of genes—probably well over 99 percent—that your enemy has, you have too. You cannot possibly be much different outside of height, weight, gender, and skin color. The rest is the result of your different family and cultural dramas. These contribute, of course, to how you see things and what you want and how you act, but not to the basic person who you are.

If you slip into your Zen Space, you will be able to appreciate the truth of the third and maybe the second point above.

§

Let me add some new thoughts here. When discussing the North Koreans above, lurking underneath was the idea of cultural difference. People from different cultures have different values, and they have different styles. For example, the common wisdom is that Asians consider it important to "maintain face" in the outcome of the bargaining. Frankly, I have never met anyone who did not need to maintain face, Asian or otherwise. That is a supposed but not real style difference. But there are certainly real ones. Companies preparing to deal with foreign businesses will often hire consultants to prepare them to meet the others part way and to be sensitive to offending.

Realistically within North American culture, which is the milieu for this book, there are—and for a long time have been—cultural differences between generations. For example, my adolescence was in the 1950s, during the evolution from black rhythm-and-blues music to a more widespread rock and roll. White parents were so angered by this music that they resorted to using political pressure and police to keep white kids from attending concerts by black performers, and black and white kids from sitting or standing in the same parts of auditoriums. They also pressured advertisers on white radio stations not to allow rhythm and blues (which were played on "race" stations) or "suggestive" white artists such as Elvis Presley. Music is a key cultural marker.

So is dress, in its broadest sense, as is using "street language" in formal situations like a negotiation. These are cross-generational differences.[3] It is

---

[3] I refer to Depression Children, or Traditionalists, born in the 1920s and 1930s; Transitionals, born 1940-1945, who choose Depression or Boomer; "Boomers," 1946-1965' "Gen-X," 1965-1979; and Gen-Y or Millennials, 1980 and later. There are great differences among writers on the date ranges. This article, http://legalcareers.about.com/od/practicetips/a/multigeneration.htm, focuses on generations as they function in law firms, but the ideas can be applied to generally working with the various generations and their values.

not always true that people of different generations will have cultural differences that lead to misunderstanding and hostility. But it is true often enough that it bears keeping it in mind.

Let me now add one more thing to be aware of, and that is style differences. People have various styles of behavior, and various psychologists and others have worked out various ways of describing the clusters they seem to fall into. You have probably heard of the Myers-Briggs personality type classification,[4] and maybe of the DISC assessment,[5] each with some 80 years of history, and each with its proponents and skeptics. Whether you fully accept either or some other typology, it seems reasonable to assume people do fall in personality clusters, and they vary a great deal in how they interact with other people.

I am not going to insert a treatise here on whether all these generational or personality clusters are real or why they happen, or any other academic stuff. I believe there is enough evidence that people are different, and different by clusters, that we need to be able to manage it. But how? More after I introduce one more idea.

The representatives or parties negotiating increasingly will cross generational lines. Similarly, representatives and parties will be of cross personality styles. In chapter four I recommended stating the needs your side has for the outcome of

---

[4] http://www.myersbriggs.org/my-mbti-personality-type/mbti-basics/ is especially helpful.

[5] **D**ominance–relating to control, power, and assertiveness; **I**nfluence–relating to social situations and communication; **S**teadiness–relating to patience, persistence, and thoughtfulness; and **C**onscientiousness–relating to structure and organization.

the negotiation—the vision. That was what I would now call a "substantive" need. But people also have *personal* needs during the process that are different from those of their counterparts and even their cohort.

For example, if it drives you nuts that someone is constantly texting or reading texts while they are at the bargaining table, ask if they could limit that to frequent breaks. But also understand they may be perfectly able to "multitask" even though you cannot. On the other hand, you might say, "I mean you no disrespect, but I hope you can accept my wearing jeans instead of a suit. They make me feel more at ease, and more open to frank discussion and resolution."

Of course, that means you are describing the personal/style things you need. How do you want to be addressed? What is important to you by way of the pace of the discussions? Dress and piercings in the bargaining room? Use of texting and "berry" devices? Coarseness of language? If you expect to spend many hours dealing with all the issues, you need to make clear each other's personal needs.

Imagine being a Boomer banker dealing with a small but growing business run by a couple of Gen-Ys to which you might loan money. Will you be put off by piercings, jeans and T-shirts, or constant texting? If so, will you blow a chance to make a productive loan by unloading criticism on them, by walking out, or by letting your personal preferences overshadow your good lending sense?

What if you are the Gen-Y? Are you put off by the Brooks Brothers suit or the three-piece lawyer the banker brought or the apparent over-attention to detail? What if the Brooks Brothers suit is on a woman? What do you do with all of these generational and personality clusters? First, simply be aware. Although people vary greatly, they do tend to cluster in their behaviors, by generation and by personality type.

Second, if you expect a long negotiation or a series of negotiations, try to adapt to the style needs of others. That does not mean change into them, anymore than you can change into a werewolf. (You can't, can you? Just checking.) It means you can anticipate reactions to what you say and do, and anticipate their behavior. It would be worthwhile to look online for material on the various named generations and about Myers-Briggs Personality Types. Knowing about them can help you understand how they are similar to you or different.

You could handle all these differences in two ways—by fighting or by accepting. That is, you could make it clear or implicit you don't like dealing with people not like you, demanding they conform to your ways. Do you think that will work well for you? Instead, if there are multiple generations or cross-types at the table, be flexible. **Expect to treat others the way they want to be treated**, not to your standard but theirs, and expect of them similar flexibility.

Put another way, the process and conditions of negotiation are just as important to negotiate, especially at the beginning, as the substantive issues. They are just as amenable to open discussion. Without open discussion, they may hide beneath the surface and constantly get in the way of negotiating what you're really there for.

§

"I just want to teach him/her a lesson." How often has that been an excuse for some kind of uncivil or devious behavior at or before a formal bargaining table or, more often, a meeting of a board or committee? It can't succeed.

We all know that beginning at the age of maybe seven or eight, the ability of outsiders to "teach a lesson" starts to reduce until by the mid-teens it is near zero and stays there. That does not mean people can't learn lessons. They certainly can, from their environments and events they experience, and many of us are still learning until the day we die. But we don't learn when others want us to but we don't want to.

A bargaining table or boardroom is an especially bad place to teach lessons. The people on the other side or in the other clique have at best a fragile trust in you. If you start "teaching lessons," you will blow that away, along with most of your chance of making a sustainable agreement.

"But what she/he said really torqued me." I am sure it did; I've been there. It's time to call on the practice you have done and get in your Zen Space. Withdraw from the immediate and be mindful. From the point of view of a wall-fly, it probably isn't you that made them say something that made you angry. They are chronically or temporarily a whack job. (In chapter seven, I will tell you more about dealing with these critters—help is on the way.) Right now, get in your Zen Space.

§

To summarize these simple but powerful ideas,

- Use your Zen Space to help you understand and to calm your fears and anxieties about your negotiating partners.
- When bargaining, always be civil, or leave the room until you can be. Get into your Zen Space ASAP.
- Keep in mind that the other folks have experienced different national and family dramas, and have different values.
- Don't try to buy off decisions based on values using money or money's worth.
- Be open and tolerant when dealing with people of different generations and different behavior styles. Negotiate about style, dress, language, and the like. Be sensitive that they may behave and communicate differently. Meet them halfway.

six

It's a Deal, Fair Thee Well

If you build every transaction and relationship in business and life with your behavior guided by the concepts of mutual benefit, fairness and truth, the profits will come. —Mitch Thrower in his "The Attention Deficit Workplace"

As I said in chapter four, few if any cultures or nations or other groups lack the notions of fairness and justice. Even individual despots and criminals will claim to be fair. Agreeing explicitly to fairness is often therefore the first thing you need to do as you begin discussions. It can start building a bridge of trust between what are often distrusting NPs. One needs little more than to simply say, "I hope and believe we can base all our discussions here on finding solutions that are fair and just to both sides." This then calls for the other side to agree or look bad. Still, what do you do now to implement that hortatory rhetoric?[1]

---

[1] I thought I would throw in a few fancy words to see if you are awake. Hortatory means "urging to some course of conduct or action" (dictionary.reference.com). Rhetoric is persuasive speech; oratory (the same).

In talking about fairness, I expect a great deal of skepticism, just as I do when I advocate getting away from demonizing and offering information instead of demanding concessions. After all, everyone knows you get what you want by demanding it and being obnoxious. As I said in chapter three, only a deal both sides are comfortable with (i.e. "sustainable") will last the time it needs to carry it out. Demanding and obnoxiousness do not help.

I expect you also to be skeptical about the benefit of getting into your Zen Space. Here is a story by Eric Stamos of zakle.com that I think illustrates the accuracy of all of these skepticisms:

Zakle.com allows people worldwide to obtain friendly favors and then pay them forward. I co-founded it.

Shortly after we launched, I met a founder of a non-profit already a household name. Its mission: helping people in several countries. He traveled the world lecturing and proudly proclaiming all the good his organization was doing.

I told him I greatly admired his dedication to doing good and all that he'd done to help so many. I then explained that our mission, too, was to help as many people around the world as possible by enabling them to find others with the skills and time needed to help them. I asked if he could introduce me to a certain company that had donated its services to his organization and routinely did so for other organizations. He flatly refused, saying too many people asked him for the same thing and he had decided to turn down all such requests. I said I understood and asked if he could at least give me a contact name and I wouldn't even mention his name when I called that person. He replied that I'd just have to find it on my own because he was too busy to look it up and email it to me.

I was in a state of shock. He had a carefully crafted image as the next Mother Theresa and turned out to be so ungenerous. I felt revolted by his hypocrisy and lack of empathy. Having succeeded he didn't give a wit about sending the elevator back down.

I went home fuming. My co-founders and I were putting in 14-hour days without a penny in salary because we believed so much in our mission of helping people. Here was this guy with his eight-figure budget, big salary, accolades, trips paid for by the organizations that asked him to speak. He had it made and we were starving and struggling and he wouldn't even throw us a stale crumb. It wouldn't have taken him more than two minutes to look up the name and email it to me.

I never admit defeat. The next morning my head had cleared and I decided I couldn't win by insisting or begging or revenge. I had an inspiration: I would do the only thing he would never expect me to do. Since he refused to help me, I would help him! We had a valuable resource that I knew he didn't have and that would benefit him greatly. I emailed him and told him that even though he couldn't help us, we wanted to help him. I explained in the email what we had to offer and how it could help his organization.

Twenty-four hours later, he replied to say he was very interested and the conversation continued from there. His organization did end up using our resource and it did help them tremendously. He felt a debt of gratitude, and we eventually got the name we were after and a few more.

After leaving his riled-up state for a calmer one—effectively, his Zen Space—Stamos stopped demonizing the other person. Now mindful, he did something to engender trust and create a moral debt. Hassled as the other fellow must have been, he nonetheless did the fair thing and returned the favor.

Another thing I said in chapter four is to avoid auctions by not stating a "position." An auction, in which the sides trade numbers, bid and asked, is fine for stock and commodity trading, but not for agreements worth negotiating. With an auction, it is going to boil down to intimidation and exchanging disparagements. ("I wouldn't give you anywhere near that much for your building—the roof leaks and it was built when Elvis was still King, before electricity." "You're just a cheap SOB who doesn't recognize intrinsic value and you're going to lose out on a great deal.") There is a better, more adult way. Almost every deal worth negotiating involves several details, maybe an interacting complex of them. That is true if it is, say, a deal for a vendor supplying a manufacturer its needs for some resource. It is also true when a non-profit board tries to plan its next year or five of activities and revenue sources, with groups of board members pushing in differing directions, or when a state legislature works on something as complex as an annual budget.[2]

If you treat a deal as having just one number at stake—something like the price of a property for sale, or the size of a state budget, or the price per widget in a "needs" contract—you are oversimplifying. You are also encouraging irrational forces that control an auction. As we have discussed, this is likely to lead to a deal that is not sustainable.

It is better to put on the table as many of the details as possible as near to the beginning as you can. By that I mean for each side to lay out its vision in detail. Talk about pricing, delivery and payment details, length of contract, mutual marketing responsibilities, and anything else that your side sees as needed in the final deal. Make it clear it is a vision or goal, and that the purpose of the negotiation is to figure a way each side can get near what it needs. Encourage your NP to similarly lay their cards on

---

[2] Most state constitutions require a balanced budget, so revenue and expenditures must add up to the same number, the size of the budget. The political parties can then conduct an auction in the media over which one delivers the most "goods" to the public with the smallest budget.

the table in detail. You don't know how much of their vision will be satisfied but there no harm in their asking.

Why should they state their needs? Because neither side has anything to lose in stating its needs. Just because it does that is no commitment by the other side to meet them. Still, it is a step toward getting together **to solve a problem that both face** and toward **treating others as equally valid people**. Substantively, negotiations in which each side treats the vision on the table as a set of mutual problems are more likely to achieve sustainable results quickly.

All this reduces the psychological need to try to "win" or "beat" your NP or view your NP as an enemy. It facilitates dealing with the easiest details—the ones not in real controversy—early on. Therefore, it creates a sense of trust between the sides. It also makes it possible for each side to make proposals that are realistic steps toward meeting their NP's needs. Maybe the proposals will be acceptable or close enough to adjust until they work. With needs on the table, there is no longer a requirement to read the other person's mind, and energy can be focused on structuring to cover as much as possible for both sides' benefit.

OK, I am aware that some people live for winning, or for beating someone else. If you are one of those, then back off. That attitude *does not produce sustainable deals*. It produces deals that go awry and end up in the hands of my brothers and sisters at the bar who do litigation—they will be happy to take money from your clients, shareholders, or your family.

If you face such a "win addict" get to your Zen Space at the beginning and make it clear your goal is a fair and sustainable deal, and if your NP does not share that, then the negotiations are over. Of course, a negotiator with the slightest experience will make it explicit that agreement on one point depends entirely on there being a complete agreement. Actually, in any negotiation, everything within reason—every requirement and expectation—should be stated explicitly. That avoids mistakes and angry debates when things look like they wrapping up.

§

Often negotiations have to deal with situations where there seems to be only so much money or other value to go around. On the surface, if one side wins, the other loses, and vice versa. Often that is because the sides do not notice a way around this "zero-sum game." There usually is one.

I am going to work through this problem using some examples. The first is dividing a budget. Let's say your organization, a non-profit or government, has limited funds this coming year, as is usually the case. You head a committee and need to negotiate with another committee about how to divide the limited funds. Of course, the instinct is to paint a picture of utter disaster for the whole organization if your committee/department does not get all it has asked for, even if that screws the other committee. The other committee's ploy is... the same disaster picture...if *their* budget is cut. What to do?

Let me climb to about 30,000 feet to deal with this. The problem is not enough money. Almost no project, task, organization, etc., has enough resources. All resources are limited. Obviously, one part of the solution is to try to use resources more efficiently. Exactly how to do that is well beyond the scope of this book. Still, there is another way.

The suggestion is not to wrestle over pie slices but to make the pie bigger. Now the problem becomes how to do that, especially if this is a non-profit. Sometimes creating a story that pulls at heartstrings more than the stories from other non-profits will work, but the public are pretty jaded. The best appeal may be to self-interest. I am no expert on fund-raising, but I will just say I have seen raffles on fancy Mercedes be quite effective in drawing attention and dollars. All you need do is find a friendly Mercedes dealer looking for some favorable publicity.

I want also to look at a different case, something more commercial. I am going to imagine being what I have always aspired to. I picture myself as a rock star,[3] negotiating with the manager of a venue over percent of the gate for a concert. (The "gate" is the total dollar volume of ticket and refreshment/extras sales for the concert.) Each side demands the bigger share, and each can make a plausible argument why it would be fair for it to get more, usually a "but for" argument. ("Without my voice you have nothing to put in your auditorium." "Without my auditorium you have no

---

[3] If you look at my picture on my website, http://negotiation-pro.com/, you will see why people say I look exactly like Jerry Garcia, but less scruffy, and I have a better singing voice. Back from the dead.

place to sing.") This presentation of arguments can lead to a great deal of time and energy spent essentially "litigating" who has a better case for getting a bigger piece of the pie. What is also going on below the surface is a reduction in the level of trust between the parties as they wrestle for the bigger slice.

Let me work a few numbers. Let us say we go with the artist/venue model, with 20,000 tickets at 100 bucks each plus 20 bucks a person in drinks, etc. That makes the gate total $2.4 million. Five percent of that—the difference between getting half the gate and 55%—is $120,000. Now let us increase the gate 10%, reasonable if both sides put their energy into flogging the concert instead of fussing with each other. That increase is $240,000 and, if divided equally is also $120,000, with much less stress and ill feeling, and a good chance of another concert next year. An extra concert, maybe a matinee, with maybe half again the gate is, if divided equally, worth an extra $600,000 to each side. How do you do this?

Let's say we are talking about a Grateful Dead concert. Jerry is really dead, with ashes spread over the Ganges and San Francisco Bay. Still, besides his music he left four daughters (with a variety of wives and girlfriends). Arrange a "special appearance" by some of the daughters. If any have musical talent they can play a number with the band, but just their coming on stage would add emotional glitter, get advance local TV and newspaper coverage, and pump up sales.[4] So, for a few

---

[4] Maybe a concert on his birthday. Perhaps some of the daughters will refuse to come if others come—there was bad blood among some of the moms. More controversy and more publicity.

bucks hire a publicist with some creativity, and think something up instead of fighting over who gets more than half.

Besides the artist/venue model, another situation where this comes up often is where a manufacturer buys a major component from a vendor, adds some value by assembly, etc., and then places product in its distribution channel. Although I do not know the details of their relationship, Intel sells processor chips to manufacturers that place them in computers. Intel does advertising to increase sales of computers based on their chips, while the manufacturers of course also advertise their specific products, always mentioning "Intel inside." This combined advertising increases the pie for Intel and the manufacturers. It is in the interest of both to maintain good relations, not animus over the price per thousand or ten thousand chips.

The thing to do, then, is to try a few numbers just as I did, and see whether fighting over a few percent on the split is as valuable as joining together to increase the total sales.

As I've said previously, moving from an adverse relationship between the sides to a joint search for creative solutions for legitimate business differences is most likely to produce a sustainable agreement and relationship.

§

What about NPs who negotiate in bad faith. There is no doubt: Some do. Chapter seven discusses Bullies, Tricksters and Nut Cases, and these bullies and tricksters do operate in bad faith. Still, right now some general advice is in order. First, take careful and accurate notes during the negotiations. If possible, bring someone along whose role is not talking but writing. If your NP demands you stop taking notes, it is time to walk away. Do it slowly enough that they have time to stop you and relent. But if they are serious that you cannot take notes, you can imagine how bad their memory will be when it is time to carry out the deal.

Some deals are not worth making. As bad as it was coming to a deal, the trouble will only get worse when the ink has dried. It takes fortitude, but also wisdom, to stop negotiating when it is clear the other side is operating in bad faith despite your pointing this out.

Still, I would not accuse your NP of bad faith or dishonesty quickly or casually. They may see things differently. Instead, point out the two versions of their statements, etc., from different times, and ask how they can be harmonized. Give them a chance to explain and/or save face. Keep an open mind, unless of course this is not the first time and the explanations have been weak.

Sometimes of course you need more than good notes and fortitude. You need to deal with nut cases, bullies, and other tricksters. You need to read the next chapter.

seven

Bullies, Tricksters, and Nut Cases

Eventually we will find (mostly in retrospect, of course) that we can be very grateful to those people who have made life most difficult for us. —Ayya Khema

Some people either act as if they are crazy, negotiate by playing tricks, or are actually a bit crazy. This makes them hard to deal with, but this chapter will make it easier. I am talking about three groups:

- the situationally neurotic
- bullies and tactical tricksters
- chronic neurotics[1]

---

[1] Some people cannot be negotiated with. They need to be treated medically. I mean psychotic or nearly psychotic people who hallucinate (they see or hear what isn't there) or are deluded (seeing what is there as something entirely different, such as a candlestick as a dagger). The other group who you should not try to negotiate with used to be called "psychopaths," people who essentially are without a conscience. (The term now used is Antisocial Personality Disorder.) You can probably make a deal with them, but they will not keep it unless it is convenient for them.

They each need very different treatment. Let's start with situational neurotics.

§

Consider this scenario: One of the kids threw up at breakfast. By the time you cleaned up, you were behind schedule. The car wouldn't start and it was raining torrentially, so taxis were running late. The big negotiation was scheduled for 10 a.m., it is 10 minutes of and the office is at least 30 minutes away. What a day.

One can imagine many other disturbing scenarios, some longer term—for example, involving terminal illness or the death of a close relative or friend.

Any of these situations can make someone crazy, and they do happen. If your NP or NP's representative acts weird—on a short fuse or a bit paranoid—and what you have heard or know about him or her says this is unusual, they are probably situationally neurotic. (If acting weird is reported to be their normal mode, then please move on to the next section of this chapter, on tricksters and bullies.)

Since they don't normally act paranoid or react weirdly to whatever someone says, the best approach is to assume that this behavior is not merely a tactic. If you don't have advance information about the person, I would give them the benefit of the doubt until you are sure otherwise. So, start by assuming their situation outside the negotiation is making them edgy or plain nuts. Recognize that is not always easy to keep your own emotions under control when you deal with someone who is not fully under control. So to stay out of your Impulse Place, please spend a moment getting into your Zen Space with the methods of chapter ywo.

Do not treat the person as an adversary but as an acquaintance. Be empathetic, trying to put yourself in their shoes. Draw out feelings gently, not by probing. They are as human as you are and we have all had bad days, bad weeks, and bad years.

"Mr. Smith, you seem edgy. Almost everything I have said to you has brought a rebuke, and that is not something I normally get from people. I am wondering if there is something going on outside this room, and that maybe we would do well to postpone today's session. I do not want to start off on the wrong foot and wreck this negotiation permanently."

Rely on your intuition. You are not a child, and you have been dealing with people for some time, starting with your parents, siblings, and cousins, and moving on to schoolmates and so forth. You know more than you think you know. So, respond to whatever the person says based on one principle. That is, you act as an adult.

Adults do not call names or accuse people. If they do not know something, they say so; they do not make things up or cover up. They do not try to bully anyone.

If you act like an adult in this way, it will give the other person a model for his or her own behavior.

They will imitate. Children, neurotic adults, bullies, and even lower primates have an impulse to imitate, and in this case you are using this inclination for a good purpose. It may take several rounds of adult conversation to make this work. Overall, your attitude should be solicitous without being patronizing—concerned for their well-being while recognizing you don't know them and cannot presume to tell them what to do. You can say they are making you feel uncomfortable, and you would appreciate either a change or a postponement.

> "I am sorry but your repeated comments about my being a liar or untrustworthy, when we have just met, make me feel uncomfortable, and I do not want to continue this way. If you have a specific problem with me, let's talk about it. If you are not feeling well, maybe we should take a break or come back another day."

Nothing in the rules of engagement of humans requires you to take abuse, and those rules do apply in negotiation, despite what you may have seen in movies or TV. And you may say so, so long as you do not accuse someone of anything. **Phrase what you say in terms of the effect on you**. That does not mean "You really piss me off," but more like, "I feel mighty uncomfortable when you repeatedly call me names."

If the person does say they are not feeling well then, again, be solicitous without being patronizing. It is perfectly OK to be human at a bargaining table. Feel confident in your intuition. If you reach the conclusion, however, that the crazy behavior is a tactic[2] or beyond their control, then move on to the next section on tactics and bullies or the later one on chronic neurotics.

§

Some people have either been trained in the *tricks and tactics school of negotiation* or by their manager to intimidate and control people, especially customers and vendors.

There are a couple dozen games and tricks; here are the most common ones:

- good cop/bad cop
- "We're good to go, I just need the boss's OK." (the "sales manager tactic")
- "That's our policy."
- "Take it or leave it."
- "The offer expires in [a short period of time]." (the "expiration game")

What do you do when you are faced with these tactics?

First, recognize someone may be trying to play you. If you feel you are being pressured or tricked, you probably are. If you hear one of the themes in the list, someone is probably trying to intimidate you. They have no right to. Negotiation is for adults.

---

[2] There is a true story later in the chapter about someone who used craziness tactically to get what they wanted. I once had a boss who I think did this, although maybe he was just nuts.

Pressure, fright, and tricks are for bullies. Bullies are people who feel they have no value themselves and must either intimidate or capitulate. You are powerful and knowledgeable, because you are reading this book and know about negotiation. You also know you can always walk away if the NP does not bargain in good faith. Intimidation tactics are not good faith. Neither are tricks.

Take a slow deep breath, in fact take a few of them, and slip into your Zen Space. Understand that they may not be tricking or pressuring you but probably are. But do not accuse them, because an undeserved accusation will poison a possible negotiation. Even an accurate charge will merely make them defensive.

Good cop/bad cop is so well known I will give just a one-sentence description. Two people alternate for the NP, one as a bully and the other as a nice person ("unbully") apologizing for the first. It is effective enough that even someone who does this for a living, like a negotiator, police officer or military interrogator, may cave in if they are the target. The bully frightens and intimidates and makes the victim feel unworthy and vulnerable. The unbully then takes advantage of the victim's feeling of weakness in the presence of the bully to close the deal on the NP's terms. Relief is the name of the game. You are so relieved the bully left the room, presumably to eat a wild boar uncooked, that you will jump at the unbully's offer.[3]

---

[3] I have never witnessed this, but have heard tell of people who can instantaneously flip from bad cop to good cop and back, saving the expense of having two cops, but with the same effect. What fantastic acting.

How do you deal with this? First, you need to recognize it for what it is. But do not accuse. Say something like:

"Wow, this feels like good cop/bad cop. I saw that on TV a couple days ago. You know what? You two are not making me feel comfortable that I should make a deal with you. How about we start over again and all try to be adults working on a problem together?"

How about **the sales manager tactic**? In large part, this is a variant on good cop/bad cop, with bad cop never leaving his office, maybe not even present. The game here is you were so relieved that the sales rep made a deal with you that you let down your guard and are blown away by the sales manger's rejection. Now, not wanting to get back into the stress of negotiating, you will take whatever they suggest.

Take a moment to get into your Zen Space. Then say something like:

"Wow, this feels like the sales manager tactic. I saw that on TV a couple days ago. Is that what you are up to? You know what? You are not making me feel comfortable I should make a deal with you. How about we start over again and you put me with someone who has the authority to make a deal. Or if he is too busy then I can come back another time or go somewhere else."

Take it or leave it and the **expiration game** are both pressure tactics. The idea with both is to make you feel you have no choice but to accept whatever they offered or be lost entirely and forever. Go for your Zen Space first.

"Wow, this feels like take it or leave it/the expiration game. I saw that on TV a couple days ago. You know what? You are not making me feel comfortable that I should make a deal with you. How about we start over again and act like adults who believe in making fair deals, as we discussed at the beginning? Or, if you have no authority to alter your policy when it needs altering, then please put me in touch with someone who can."

There are almost 20 more tactics, all designed to intimidate, make you feel unworthy, make you feel you cannot win and that you must do it their way. So, what then? There is no reason to memorize twenty specific responses. Instead, try a polite but firm parry:

"I don't know just why you are saying that or whether you are running a game on me, although I saw something like this on TV once [describing]. In any case, it will not get us closer to solving our problem. So let's focus on our needs and how close we can get to satisfying both yours and mine with a fair bargain."

You have not accused. You have raised a question. Most people who are being tricky do not like it noticed and will move on to a different attitude. If they persist, maybe with another trick, then you always have the option to take a break in the negotiations or actually terminate.

"That's our policy," by the way, usually comes from specific 'customer disservice' (i.e., manipulation) training. One book I read on dealing with this had the author outsmarting the policy, although with a soupçon of outsmart-the-employee. Why bother? Ask for the manager or go elsewhere. If the manager comes, then insist on a fair solution, which they will usually agree is appropriate.

§

Usually what seems like a tactic is a tactic, and what seems like just craziness is just that, but not always. You may need to make subtle distinctions, relying on your intuition. This story is from Andrew Cagnetta of Transworld Business Brokers, TWorld. com:

A seller was absolutely a crazed lunatic through a deal. Blow up on the phone, hang up, leave meetings, told the buyers at one point "Go home Harvard Scum" while on the phone with them as they sat outside his offices after flying in from California to speak with him. He eventually cut off everyone from communication a couple of weeks prior and we never knew if he was going to show up to the closing.

I speculated out loud that he must be either a crazy man or will look at me at the closing and say "Cagnetta, now that's how you negotiate." We didn't have an in person closing, and after the monies were wired the phone rang. It was the seller, offering his apologies for his "antics" as they were his way of getting what he wanted.

Without being there, I would be hard pressed to know if this was a trick, as the seller portrayed it, or his normal behavior, learned over a long period as the means to always get his way. It may not matter, as we shall see.

§

Although there are a wide variety of chronic neuroses, two of them stand out as making negotiation and life in general difficult: the screamer and the victim. Almost everyone I have ever asked has had or known a screamer boss, and many of us have dealt with (or tried) to deal with people who act the victim. Each responds to a specific treatment.

From what I can tell, parents who cave in to a screaming three year old (or thereabouts) and do it consistently do the child no good. If it works once for the child, it will happen again. If the second time, there will be a third, and so on. And so this person arrives eventually at adulthood. Here is the thing. They know what they are doing. If they screamed at their teachers and bosses, they would end up suspended from school and fired from jobs.

They do not. They can control themselves, if they choose to, and you need to help them choose.

Most often, this happens in a boss-employee situation, so I am going to focus on that, although you can adapt it to a vendor-customer situation, for example.

You have a boss who continually screams at you. Probably he does this with other employees as well, but you can only deal with the problem as it affects you. Make an appointment to see the boss. Prepare by listing on paper all the good things you bring to the table and that will disappear if you leave. (In a prior chapter, we discussed the importance of research and preparation before negotiating, and this is an example.) Spend the time needed to make the list, but also visualize quitting, so it will seem less scary if you have to do it. Now, spend a few minutes in your Zen Space preparing just before the appointment:

> "I have been working for you now for [X weeks / months / years], and during that time you have consistently screamed at me when simple discussion would have been enough. While you are my supervisor, that does not entitle you to engage in abusive volume, accusations, or language. It is your obligation to act like an adult and, indeed, your doing that would make you a more effective supervisor.

> "As your employee, I do these various tasks and do them well:

- A
- B
- C
- ...

"If you do not stop your verbal abuse, I will have no choice but to resign and to do so at the point where I can no longer abide the abuse. You will then need to find someone else to do these tasks and also tolerate the abusive tone and words. What, [sir/madam], is your reply?"

If you have made your case well, after a few moments of thought they will promise to change their behavior. They will, because they do not want lose a good employee. They will, because they are merely doing habitual behavior that surrounds a core person who feels impotent. And finally, they will because they have always had the ability to turn it off. If he or she did not, but instead screamed at anyone they did not like or who upset them, they would be in jail for disorderly conduct, not occupying a boss's chair. Of course, they may think that they do not scream—or that they have the right to.[4]

Years ago, when I was a green lawyer, I had a screamer boss. He was so apparently out of control that he screamed at his own wife when she came in periodically to do the books. Just by accident, I came

---

[4] My wife's boss's boss was like that, a screamer. She stood up to him and he backed down, although he still screamed at everyone else when the fancy took him.

on the method I just outlined and confronted him. He promised to control himself, but it was finally too much for him. He tried but could not keep up adult behavior, so I quit and started working for myself. A few weeks later he phoned sheepishly and asked if I would come back. We negotiated terms, and I did come back for awhile until I got a better job. He behaved himself. I did eventually leave, but from time to time, he phoned with a question or something and was usually whisper quiet. Screamers can always control themselves one customer at a time. It will not be easy, and they may seek help from a therapist to get rid of a bad habit, but they can do it.

What about the "victim," the person to whom everything bad is always happening and who needs a rescuer, namely you? For one thing, they are harder to spot. Sometimes a pile of awful drops on someone. That can confuse you into thinking they really are accident prone, but after awhile, your intuition tells you otherwise. Although adults do the best they can, with a little help from their friends, victims are incapable, entreating favors on the basis they cannot survive without.

This again is habitual behavior. When they played victim as a child, their parents were always rescuing, so now they play victim and recruit rescuers. Anyone can be a victim of one burglary, for example, but no one is a victim of an unending series of mishaps that they can never handle. Victims find it useful to see the world as full of traps that always ensnare them, so they cannot get out of them and they need your help to survive. How do you handle them?

You keep in mind that you are not responsible (unless, of course, you are a firefighter and their house is on fire). In a bargaining session, your responsibility certainly is to yourself or your constituency.

Victim: "But if I don't get this sale and make a profit, my boss is going to fire me and then I won't be able to pay the mortgage and my kids will be on the street."

You: "I am sorry about that, but it is not my problem. I can give you the sale, but I am going to have to get something in return, such as a discounted price. My responsibility is to my company."

If this does not get through immediately and they persist, you will need to resort to what used to be called "broken record," when music came from circular vinyl platters called records. (I suppose now it should be "dirty DVD.") How it works is, no matter what "button" she or he presses, your response is "I am sorry, but my responsibility is to my company, and I can only give you a sale if you give me a discount."

Debbi Mack, a Maryland lawyer and writer, told me about her encounter with an opposing lawyer who oscillated between screamer and victim. Ms. Mack had obtained a money judgment—a court decision that his client owed her client a specific amount of money. While such a judgment does not allow for threatening jail unless the defendant pays, it does enable other remedies. One is a garnishment.[5] It turns out the defendant had made a small payment against the judgment with a check, so Ms. Mack had an idea where to look for more money. She filed for and got a garnishment on the bank where the check was payable. Now the fun began. As she tells it:

> The defendant's lawyer filed a motion to vacate the base judgment and remove the garnishment, claiming the underlying judgment was obtained by fraud. Since I had not been involved in getting the judgment, I knew only that there had been no agreed conditions on collecting it. And I knew of no evidence of wrongdoing. Defendant claimed to have agreed to the judgment based on verbal assurances made about enforcing it, but none of that matters legally. So the law and facts were completely on my side.
>
> After the debtor's attorney filed his motion he called me from time to time to harangue me, call me names, yell at me, plead and beg, etc., etc. When he asked, "How can we settle this matter? We shouldn't have to go to court over this," I said, "I completely agree. This doesn't belong in court. And we can settle the matter, if your client will withdraw this motion and pay what's owed in full." In other words,

---

[5] In effect, a garnishment is a claim that the bank, which owes the defendant money—the money defendant deposited—should instead pay the plaintiff, a lawsuit within a lawsuit.

I never let him rattle me, never gave an inch, because it was ridiculous to do so (if not unethical and outright malpractice).

So...in the end, the debtor did agree to pay the full amount.

Here, the opposing counsel used a combination of (screamer) haranguing, name calling, pleading and begging (victim-like), trying to cut down on what his client legally owed. Ms. Mack stuck to her guns, pointed to the facts, and eventually got all her client's money for him.

§

So dealing with bullies, tricksters and neurotics is a matter of knowing a few basic parries, how and when to use them, and always being ready to slip into your Zen Space to ward off the fright and anxiety in favor of repose and confidence.

eight

Negotiate with Your Constituency

[Y]ou must unite your constituents around a common cause and connect with them as human beings. —James Kouzes and Barry Posner

If you are negotiating, you almost certainly have some constituency—voters, clients, union members, a faction you belong to of a board of directors, your spouse, your neighbors, and so forth.

Legislators have voters imploring them one way or the other and threatening to withhold support next election or even put up an opponent. If this is a town or city council or board, it can get ugly. (I have been there. Trust me.)

Union officials often are in a vise between members who want on the one hand to beat the heck out of the management SOBs, and members on the other hand who want labor peace and no strike. Each side threatens to vote the officials out or worse.

Lawyers sometimes have clients who see negotiation in the same light as litigation, namely as a fight rather than a way to avoid a costly litigation.

You might find yourself a member of one faction of a board of trustees who sits down with a leader from the opposing faction to try to restore a little civility, remove impasse, and encourage forward progress. The rest of your faction wants you to stand fast ("on principle") and make no compromise, while compromise is the only way to have the board move on.

In dealing with your constituency, you really have a second negotiation process to deal with. The key is that your constituents will normally not be in the primary negotiation, but they will be able to demand concessions and negotiation strategies in advance and question the result afterward. To do that requires only strong lungs. Your job as negotiator is to communicate, communicate some more, and then even more. You need to discuss:

- With your constituents: what you expect the other side's vision to be (and later, what it is)
- With your constituents: the extent to which the NP's vision can be harmonized with your side's vision without great harm to either.
- With your constituents: realistically what the strengths and weaknesses are of your side and the NP's.
- With the NP: your constituency's vision[1]

---

[1]Just as a reminder, the NP, or negotiating partner, as used in this book is the other side of the table, not the people on your side or your constituents. From the context I will make clear whether I am talking about all of them or just their representative(s).

Once you have done all this with your constituents, only then can you communicate it to your NP.

You need to do a good deal of active listening, by which I mean listening without focusing on what you are going to say next, but instead taking notes and asking clarifying questions. Still, eventually you must cut off discussion when nothing new is being exposed—it's just repetition so everyone gets a chance to talk (and bore others).

Depending on the duration of your relationship, there should be some trust established with your constituents. You will have learned just how much to pass on about what the other side has said—not all. The derogatory personal comments of the NP's representative, for example, should not go further than the negotiation table. However, all the NP's proposals and responses to your proposals do need to be passed to your constituents, as rapidly and accurately as you can, no matter whether they are attractive, insulting, or somewhere in the middle. Anything else invites suspicion that you, their representative, are selling them out.[2] With suspicion comes distrust and a downhill spiral of the relationship, regardless of whether fees or salaries have been paid you.

§

Someone suggested to me that while talking with your constituents, you should not share your view of what their vision ought to be or try to influence

---

[2] If the negotiation is not going well, there is always the tendency, anyway, to kill the messenger.

them. The idea is it needs to be their vision—you should not interfere.

Here is my view. If the vision is for their own use—a vision for a group's own future, like what the hospital will look like in five or ten years—then I agree. A facilitator helping them formulate the vision should not impose his or her own views.[3] But if the vision is for use in a negotiation, then the representative should not bite their tongue but should offer input on what is realistic. For example:

- If the group is Mr. and Mrs., planning to sell their house, certainly the real estate agent should talk about comparables and recent market trends.
- If the group is a patient and family, the physician should certainly talk about realistic treatment plans, and their pros and cons.
- If the group is a union, the union leader should influence discussion of what vision he or she should present to management next month, not let the members "blue sky" a vision that is so far out it may lead management to infer wrongly that the union would really prefer a strike to a deal.

§

---

[3] The hospital board certainly needs input from health planners, finance people, real estate people, and land-use lawyers and the other professionals I apologize to for not mentioning.

In my own negotiation consultancy, I was contacted by a couple of middle managers whose new CEO demanded every company cost be reduced by five percent. They wanted my help in dealing with a software company whose product was critical to company operations and that wanted to make a five percent increase in annual maintenance. Of course, the middle managers had little leverage. They could simply cut off maintenance entirely, or threaten to. Still, what would happen when and if they needed support? They could try to make a deal for "as needed" support, and might get it, but at low priority ("after we respond to everyone else"). They might as well have been asking the power company for a five percent discount as a modest customer with nowhere else to go for electricity.

What I did point out was that they needed to negotiate with the new CEO, to point out that vendors were not all interchangeable. Some needs could be gotten from several sources, allowing for pitting one against another, but some things like software support, electric power, and the services of a law firm (ahem) familiar for years with their circumstances and needs might be sole source. My understanding is they were able to make the CEO as their constituent understand this. They paid my invoice promptly and didn't ask for five percent off.

They needed to communicate with their constituent the consequences of blindly applying the five percent reduction rule to a sole-source utility vital to the company's operation. Once they communicated, they were able to do what they needed to.

Before beginning the process, you need to set reasonable expectations, even at the risk of being fired. You need to make sure your constituents' collective vision is aligned with the vision you voice to the NP. That means you need your constituents to agree on a collective vision. You also have to set your own expectation for yourself: that sometimes your constituents, especially the most vocal of them, will accuse you of selling out. This is painful but true, and best met aware.

What should be your process? If you have a single constituent or a unified group, negotiate with them just as if they were an NP, using all you have learned in the previous chapters, and come to an agreed vision you can go ahead with. Make sure they understand the WHO (What Happens Otherwise). Do not, however, allow constituents to get used to the idea of your being a hired gun sworn to follow their commands. Liberate them from it.

They have presumably hired you for your experience, intelligence, and reliability, and they need to be reminded of that from time to time. If you have no expertise, why did they make you their rep? That means it is perfectly OK to question the constituents' visions, be it one client or a hall full of them. This is true whether you are lawyer, legislator, or leader of a faction. Remember that it is not OK for the vision to be of something unethical, illegal, immoral, or unattainable.

If there are factions among your constituents, become a mediator and let them ventilate first. Then bring them to a common vision, influenced by your expert view of what is possible and what is your side's negotiating strength compared with that of the NP. Bring them to common vision through a negotiation you guide them through.

A few words about legislators: In all democratic republics—where democratically elected representatives act for the electors—there is a tension. This is the conflict between acting for the vision of your constituents, or the vision of the entity as a whole, or the benefit of either.

For example, let us say you are the senator for the first district in your state senate. Do you blend and adopt the vision of the people of the first district? Or combine and stand for the vision of the people of the entire state? Or do you act for your own vision of the first district, or of the entire state? I do not think there is a right answer. People have been debating this since there have been elected representatives. All I can say is what long-lasting politicians know: Do your best to make these interests all coincide by a mixture of listening, explaining, and persuading. Help to mold the visions, if possible, into one. (And publicly muddy the differences.)

Finally, here is a revelation to clients and constituents: Your reps are not robots. Representatives get closer together personally than their clientele do to each other. The reps live the hours and perhaps days of back-and-forth bargaining, sometimes in discomfort, usually in stress. They have less emotional baggage involved than do their constituents, often much less, and often have had prior encounters. In fact, this comradery enables some of the mutual reaching out for common ground and eventual compromise.

They mostly operate outside the watching and hearing of the constituents. That means they may share an occasional story in which one makes his or her own constituent the butt of a joke, or otherwise disparages their own constituent. Sometimes they listen to their opposite number, the NP's rep, and agree to a concession simply because it is the right thing to do, inviting a similar concession. Constituents do not engage or elect representatives to beat up people they disagree with. They engage and elect envoys to make things like deals happen. If you are such a representative, you need to keep that in mind, especially when your constituents seem to be gripped by a mad orgy of groupthink. Keep communicating with your people, and do not hesitate to do your job and make a deal.

nine

Summation

*In three words I can sum up everything I've
learned about life: it goes on.* —Robert Frost

Everyone will tell you, "Take a deep breath before
you answer." If what you are answering is
threatening, infuriating, or otherwise going to make
you say something stupid, this is sound advice. It
has been forever.

Applied to negotiating, you cannot negotiate
successfully when you are emotionally off, but you
can control your state—get to your Zen Space—by
breath and muscle exercises. They are outlined
in chapter two. If you are emotionally out of balance—in your Impulse Place as we have called
it—you will be using the part of the brain that has
evolved over millions of years and thousands of
predecessor species to choose between fighting,
fleeing, and hiding. This part is hardly suited for
the nuanced weighing of your negotiation partner's
maneuvers and proposals, let alone those of your
own constituents. The part of the brain that does
those comparisons of risks and rewards is much

more recently evolved.[1] And it corresponds physically to your Zen Space.

So **practice getting to your Zen Space** easily and anytime you need it, as if you were Clark Kent ducking into a phone booth to become Superman®.

OK, so now you are ready emotionally. What can you do to make sure your side "wins"? Winning a negotiation in the terms most people think of—getting the best of the other side—is shortsighted. Almost every deal requires at least one round (if not more) of delivery by each side. The simplest version would be one side paying money and the other delivering goods.[2] With either multiple rounds or just one, the side that thinks it was taken can screw up the deal by delaying or delivering bad goods or a thousand other tricks. The urge for revenge in humans is very strong.

Instead, the goal of negotiation, in general, should be a **sustainable deal**—a deal that both sides think is **fair**, if not all they wanted. They will then be motivated to complete the deal in its own terms, with no passive aggression or tricks, because they want the same themselves, and because they recognize the value of establishing long-term business relations.

Still of course, you need a specific goal. You need (with your constituents) to draw up a vision of how the deal would go if you got all you want. Your

---

[1] In chapter one I spoke of the separate parts. The later evolution of the risk/reward part is in Appendix A.
[2] Each side could be delivering goods, but different goods—a barter.

vision is what a good settlement would look like to your side. Talking about it gives the NP an idea of what points are important to you. It is not the same as a negotiating "position," as people often call it. A "position" is a kind of demand—"Unless we get this, there will be no deal."

A position invites an auction type of negotiation, in which the sides take turns bad-mouthing the other's recent proposal and praising their own, focusing on price rather than the totality of the deal. It also invites some hostility instead of cooperation toward finding common ground.

As I said in chapter four:

- Gain as much information as you can about the negotiating partner.
- Exchange visions for a good result with your counterparts. Announce no "position."
- Agree to work for fairness in the result.
- Avoid the two monsters of fearing you will anger the NP with too much persistence, and your own constituents with too little.
- Remain aware of the WHO—What Happens Otherwise.
- Avoid demonizing each other and maintain civility.
- Work together to form an agreement that as much as possible includes the points of both the visions.

Be strategic: make your brushstroke strategy fulfill your goal, and adopt no tactic that does not support that strategy, no matter how cool or easy to do or otherwise attractive it may seem.

Avoiding demonizing, and working together toward a solution take us back to the starting point of the book. That is, if you use the simple Zen techniques of chapter two, you will be able to see the process almost as would a fly on the wall. You will see the merits of the NP's vision—not just for them, but also for your side. True, their vision is not perfect, but neither is it completely flawed; neither are your vision and the reasons for it completely correct.

When you find your Zen Space, you will realize your NP has foibles but is not the devil in human clothing. Though it is possible, it is unlikely that they have been intentionally lying to you and maybe anyone else who will listen. More likely, they have hoodwinked themselves, or you have deluded yourself. Maybe there is some history or emotional baggage they carry that you do not know and should learn during your research about your NP.

Or you might just ask them about previous experiences relevant to the current negotiation. Just because you listen to someone, and even understand what they are saying and why they say it, that does not mean you agree with them.

One thing that often causes friction between negotiators is that they are from different generations, with different cultures, almost as if from different nations. Or they might have different personality types and see the world differently. Any of these situations warrant spending some time working out a middle ground on the process of negotiation. It could save time and anger later.

Certainly do not try to use the context of a negotiation to "teach a lesson." It will not work, and it will fracture the negotiation process. No one wants to be taught a lesson.

Many people find it self evident that the way to negotiate for what you want is to be demanding, obnoxious, and even threatening.[3] People who are not self-confident can be manipulated in that way. But people who have read and understood this book cannot be, nor can most experienced negotiators.

A more effective technique is to build some trust across the table, get agreement that a fair deal is in everyone's interest, and then go on to try to meld two different visions into a single vision that works reasonably well for both. And get things into your own notes as quickly as you can, because human memory is very fallible.

Some negotiations seem to be about "zero sum games"—about dividing a pie with just so much fruit, no more. They are especially difficult deals because no one wants the smaller piece of the pie. And there often seems little else to throw in to compensate.

One way out is not to take for granted that the pie cannot grow, and to agree to work together to make it grow, while agreeing to an even division. Also, it is often not a good business deal. That is, working together to increase the pie say five percent may put more money in your pocket than increasing

---

[3] Actor William Shatner has made a new career for himself behaving that way in ads for Priceline.com. But he is acting.

your own share from 50 to 55 percent. And cost less in time and stress.

Of course, one must be on guard against people who act in bad faith in negotiating. Most frequently this is by fabricating what you or they said at the table. Make sure someone on your side of the table takes careful and complete notes, especially if you have discovered in your research you are dealing with such a person. If they say you cannot take notes, as it insults them, pick up your papers and walk out. If you made a deal it would become the deal from hell.

Some NP representatives are very hard to deal with. Sometimes it is because they are having a bad day, week, or stretch of time. The best way to handle them—if this behavior is outside what you believe is normal for them—is to treat them like a friend or acquaintance. Imagine it is a tavern or party, not a bargaining room. Lend an ear, not unsolicited advice.

On the other hand, there are specific tactics some negotiators use to "play" their NPs. Good cop/bad cop is so well known it is almost a joke, but is often used anyway. The "sales manager game" ("my sales manager would not approve and insisted that ...") is almost as common, especially with car dealers.

There are specific parries outlined in chapter seven for these, but if you cannot recall them, try this:

"I don't know whether you are trying to play a game here, although it does remind me of something I saw on TV recently, but either way it doesn't change my mind and reduces my trust level. It makes our negotiation more unlikely to succeed."

These tactical people don't like to be found out, and may be put off enough to behave themselves. Just keep in mind that:

- Your intuition that you are being played is probably correct.
- You don't need to make a deal with someone who wants to play you; besides, they may not keep the deal once it is inked.

More difficult are some chronically neurotic people, especially two kinds, the screamers and the victims. Screamers...well...scream at everyone to unnerve them and get their way ("I'll give you what you want, just go away and leave me alone.").

Don't scream back. They are more practiced and so they are louder, and it just annoys everyone else in the room. Instead, act like an adult. Be factual, like Mr. Spock or Mr. Data. Point out what you offer in the continuing relationship pr the deal being negotiated, and ask quietly...really quietly... hat they quiet down. They probably will, albeit for you and no one else.

Victims are almost the opposite, non-agressive to the point of cowering and begging for your help, even though your helping them will hurt you or your constituents. Calmly, in adult tones, point out you have no obligation to rescue them, no matter how much rescue they seem to need, but you will do a deal with them if what you get out of it is worthwhile. No free-bies. Oops, freebies are exactly what "victims" are looking for and are accustomed to. Make clear, without judgment, that they are not available.

Much of the time when you negotiate it will be in behalf of constituents. They will be paid clients, a faction in a group or board, an entire organization, a union, a management committee, or whatever. You owe them some duties, and they owe you some, and you need to settle these at the beginning, by having a negotiation.

1. They need to pay serious attention to your advice about what is realistically possible.
2. They need to stick to the vision they give you to work for.
3. They need to leave tactical decisions to you and not second guess, nor require you to do or say anything you believe is unethical, illegal, or unnecessarily uncivil.
4. You need to stay in constant contact and be open with them about offers and visions on the table from both sides.
5. You need to listen carefully when you meet your side, not just give advice.
6. Ultimately, you need to make clear to the NP when your hands have been tied by your constituents; and to make it clear to the constituents that you will tell that to the NP.
7. You need to keep confidential what is told you by the other side explicitly or implicitly

in confidence; the latter certainly includes bad mouthing individuals on your side.

If your side can accept these reasonable ground rules, it will go well in their relationship with you. Of course, the most important of these will be item one on the list. You are engaged to make a deal, not beat up the NP, teach lessons, or anything else.

"You hired me/asked me to make a deal for you with the other side, nothing else. I am going to try my best to do just that."

And that sums up what a dealmaker—a negotiator—does.

If you want to see what they don't do, catch a Priceline commercial with William Shatner.

[Insanely wild applause]

Appendix A

Two Brains in a Box: A Possible Scientific Basis of Zen Space

The universe is full of magical things patiently waiting for our wits to grow sharper. —Eden Phillpotts, A Shadow Passes

In the past five or ten years, neuroscience has had the opportunity to study the human brain using a technology called functional Magnetic Resonance Imaging, or fMRI. With it, one can make pictures of the brain. These pictures reveal which parts are most involved with a particular processing task by measuring the use of oxygen by parts of the brain.

Brain mapping has been around for about 100 years, usually done by attaching electrodes to cat brains (at the scalp or more invasively) and then subjecting the animal to various sensory experiences, such as lights and sounds. These produced a reasonably complete set of maps of the resulting electrical activity, although not in the geometric and time detail now possible with fMRI. Moreover, the tasks one can involve a cat in do not extend to asking questions or having the cat make choices. (If you have never hosted a cat, please trust me.) Then again, electrodes have been implanted in awake and behaving monkeys, with much learned from these experiments.

A good deal was also learned from studying the effects of brain lesions—from disease and trauma: What functions did the patient lose compared with a normal patient?

Still, with its precise detail in time and space, fMRI has now become the gold standard for many scientists. Functional MRI imaging uses magnetic fields to "light up" brain tissue and to highlight what parts have a lot of oxygen-rich blood (as opposed to oxygen-poor blood). Soon after there is a burst of brain activity in an area, that area gets a dose of extra rich blood, and that gets displayed in the fMRI. Put it altogether, and you can display which area of the brain carried out a task one to five seconds ago.

Current technology allows resolving areas of the brain just 2-4 mm (1/12-1/6 in.) in diameter, sometimes less, in pictures taken just a second or two apart. And one can synchronize these "movies" with an audio track of instructions given the subject.

The major downside is that the data have to be massaged (smoothed over time and space) by software quite a lot to compensate for what engineers call "noisy" signals, and the massaging can cause spurious results. Still, fMRI is much better than the electrical mapping previously used.

But with a human volunteer quite complex tasks can be assigned while the subject is inside the fMRI machine. Since no incisions or electrodes or other invasions are needed, subjects are more readily available.

Before we discuss the results, we need to talk about some of the parts of the brain. Let us start with the amygdalae, which are two almond-shaped (amygdala means "almond shaped") brain parts located about halfway fore-and-aft in complex vertebrates. They are near the midline—the line between the right and left hemispheres. And from top to bottom, each amygdala lies far down, near the brain stem (where the brain connects through the cerebellum to the nerves going down the spine). They are in the "temporal lobes."

All mammals have temporal lobes. From the point of view of evolution, the temporal lobes have been around a long time. That is, simpler animals that have any brain at all, such as birds, apparently do have temporal lobes or quite similar structures with similar functions. At least that is the view adopted by bird neurologists the past few years. These lobes are involved with processing input from senses such as sound and vision and scents.

Interestingly, speech—both making and interpreting—is associated with the temporal and frontal lobes, but this is a function that only humans have. (Some birds have very complex ability to learn and produce hundreds of "'songs," which they seem to use for communication between them, but they do not speak.) This has led some scientists to conclude recently that nature has recycled longstanding areas of the temporal lobe, such as "Broca's area," into the service of speech.

The amygdalae have long been known to be associated with emotions and emotional memories. Fight or flight reactions appear to start from the amygdalae—freezing, rapid heartbeat, rapid breathing, and so on. We know some of this because damage to the amygdalae interferes with Pavlovian fear conditioning. (Alas, many cats and dogs suffered much fright and damage so humankind could learn about amygdalae.) Some believe the simplest animals with amygdalae use them to decide when to become fearful and what actions to take then.

Functionality that is more sophisticated has developed in vertebrates that are more complicated. Besides the amygdalae, each of us humans, as mammals, normally also has two "frontal lobes," one on each side. They are at the front of the brain, and on the top side. In general, the frontal lobes are involved with executive functions—complex decision-making, including figuring out long-term consequences and weighing risk and reward. In humans, some scientist believe the frontal lobes do not fully develop until about age 25. That may explain why adolescents and young adults take risks older people avoid.

To an extent neurologists have not yet fully resolved, the brains of all vertebrates—whether birds, lower mammals, or primate mammals like us—have a surrounding part called the cerebral cortex. (A cortex is a husk or shell.) Neurologists and others believe the cerebral cortex in humans plays a key role in memory, attention, perceptual awareness, thought, language, and consciousness. It or parts of it are believed to be involved in the slower, more reflective type of decision-making.

Like much else in the brain, the cerebral cortex is divided in parts, one of which is the orbitofrontal cortex, or OFC. This part is at the front of the head, between the orbits or cavities of the eyes. That much is certain, but some of the rest is not. Various scientists have associated the OFC with decision-making, expectation, planning, weighing of reward and punishment, and weighing sensory inputs. Also, it seems this applies also to lower primates and even rodents.

While much is known, much detail is not. The OFC studies by fMRI seem to show the OFC involved in a combination of risk-reward analysis and scent detection. The former is deliberative, but we know smells are strongly associated with emotional responses.

While the imaging data support for two systems is still vague, there is also much older behavioral evidence for multi-system decision-making. It does not point to specific places in the brain, but makes clear from psychological experiments that intuitive and affective (emotion- and mood-based) decision-making is far more rapid than, albeit not so "rational" or analytic as, the slower, more reflective system. It takes, for example, as little as one or two tenths of a second to make decisions on trustworthiness from pictures of people.

Another source of information besides experiments is from brain lesions. That is, for example, people with lesions (injuries from disease or trauma) to parts of the pre-frontal cortex suffer in their ability to make deliberative decisions.

§

Early in the twentieth century, Sigmund Freud described a theory of the unconscious that tried to put together the ancient thoughts about decision-making process that we have discussed with then recent neurological studies about functions of parts of the brain. He described what we call in English the "Id," "Ego," and "Super-ego."

These are actually bad translations of his German (Das Es, Das Ich, und Das Über-Ich); better would be the It, the I, and the Over-I. The It contains drives, pleasure seeking and emotion, and probably corresponds with the amygdalae. (Freud did not make neurological identifications, instead only trying to make a separation of the thinking process, parallel to what the neurologists were doing anatomically.) The I deals with intellectual and executive functions and may correspond with the OFC mentioned a moment ago.

The Over-I seems to be a counter-balance to the It, serving to say "No" to pleasure seeking and so forth. Perhaps its functions belong just as much in the amygdalae as the It. Fear of pleasure may be just as much an emotional response as seeking it.

Freud's triad appears to be experiencing a rebirth in view of modern neuroscience, at least to the extent of neuroscience supporting The It (Id), and The I (Ego). For about 100 years science has been trying to harmonize ancient intuitive ideas with physical findings that have come out over about the same time.

§

What are the intuitive ideas? These were what you will recall being discussed in chapter one. As stated there, over thousands of years people have been meditating as a means to more fully understanding their worlds by blocking out as best they can the physical world and the emotions, feelings, and moods that they believe interfere with real understanding.

Scientific evidence from electrode brain mapping, from seeing the results of lesions, and more recently from fMRI imaging, all point to the idea that wherever they exactly are in the brain, there are two brain systems for decision-making. We do not yet know how much they are concentrated in separate parts of the brain or how connected the systems are. So much more imaging and other work needs to be done. But so far, whether fortuitous or real, the evidence seems to be that the intuitive separation of the brain into two systems for decision-making is matched by physical separation.

For Futher Study

- Robert Pirsig, *Zen and the Art of Motorcycle Maintenance*, 0060589469 (2006 paperback, hardback was 1974)
- Eric Berne, *Games People Play*, 0345410033 (1996 Paper, Hardback was 1964.)
- Thomas Harris, *I'm OK, You're OK*, 0060724277 (orig. 1969)
- Shapiro and Jankowski, *The Power of Nice*, 0471293776 (1998)
- Shapiro and Jankowski, *Bullies, Tyrants and Impossible People*, 1400050111 (2005)
- Fisher and Ury, *Getting to Yes*, 0140157352 (1991)
- Gary Marcus, *Kluge: The Haphazard Evolution of the Human Mind*, 0618879641 (2008) or 054723824X (2009 paper)
- Sanfey and Chang, *Multiple Systems in Decision Making*, Ann. N.Y. Acad. Sci. 1128: 53062 (2008); and other works of Alan G. Sanfey.
- *About the Amygdala* found at http://www.whalenlab.info/About%Amygdala.html
- *Cerebellum lobes (illustration)* found at http://en.wikipedia.org/wiki/File:Illu_cerebrum_lobes.jpg
- Daniel C. Krawczyk, *Contributions of the prefrontal cortex to the neural basis of human decision making*, Neuroscience and Biobehavioral Reviews 26: 631-664 (2002)

About the Author

Philip L. Marcus has been an attorney and business owner for over 35 years, and during all that time has been negotiating for others or his own businesses. He received his SB and SM in engineering from MIT and a JD from the University of Maryland Law School.

Mr. Marcus is also an experienced adult trainer in various subjects that range from computer engineering to negotiating. This book evolved from seminars he has given to professional and business groups and at MIT the past five years.

He lives in Columbia Maryland with his wife Peg and their two cats.

Index

D

dance, the — 43, 48, 49.
deep breaths — 23, 26, 56.
defensive — 53, 62, 88.
demonizing — 36, 72, 74, 109, 110.
DISC — 65.
discounted utility model — 13.
distrust — 15, 101.
DPRK. *See* North Korea.

E

economists — 13, 14.
emotions — 5, 7, 8, 11, 85, 119, 123.
epinephrine — 22, 36, 37, 56, 100, 109.
expected utility model — 13.

F

fairness — 36, 41, 46, 47, 71, 72, 109.
fear — 7, 122.
fear of uncertainty — 15.
fMRI — 117, 118, 121, 123.
Freud, Sigmund — 121, 122.
functional Magnetic Resonance Imaging. *See* fMRI.

G

games — 12, 13, 87, 111.
Gen-Y — 64, 66.
generations — 64, 65, 67, 69, 110.
good cop/bad cop — 31, 87, 89.
Google — 24, 34, 38.

H

hostility — 50, 55, 62, 65, 109.

neurotic — 83, 84, 86, 113.
Northern Ireland — 44, 45.
North Korea — 58, 59, 60.
NP. *See* negotiating partner.
Nuland, M.D., Sherwin — 24.

O

Olteanu, Catalin — 48.
oxygen — 23, 26.

P

panic — 19.
parts of the brain — 10, 117, 119, 122, 123.
reflective — 10, 18, 19, 21, 25, 52, 56.
reflexive — 10, 18, 19, 21, 25, 52, 56.
passive aggressive — 31.
patience — 8, 39, 45, 48, 65.
personality types — 110.
pie — 78, 79, 80, 111.
position — 9, 23, 36, 39, 40, 41, 74, 109.
Presley, Elvis — 64.
process — 4, 47, 51, 66, 67, 100, 104, 110, 111, 122.
progressive muscle relaxation — 23, 26, 56.

Q

R

reflective. *See* parts of the brain: reflective.
reflexive. *See* parts of the brain: reflexive.
relaxed state — 25, 27.
rhythm-and-blues — 64.
rock and roll — 64.

W

Waldock, Marlene — 46.

war — 5, 52, 59.

Web — 21, 47.

What Happens Otherwise. *See* WHO.

WHO — 36, 51, 52, 53, 104, 109.

X

Y

Z

Zen — 1, 5, 7, 9, 10, 11, 16, 17, 19, 21, 23, 24, 27, 28, 40, 51, 52, 53, 56, 57, 58, 61, 62, 63, 68, 69, 72, 74, 77, 85, 88, 89, 90, 93, 98, 107, 108, 110, 117, 125.

Zen Space — 1, 7, 9, 10, 17, 19, 21, 23, 24, 27, 28, 40, 51, 52, 53, 56, 57, 58, 61, 62, 63, 68, 69, 72, 74, 77, 85, 88, 89, 90, 93, 98, 107, 108, 110, 117.

zero-sum game — 77.